£4.50

12840
338·47663

D1440321

LIBRARY
LLANDRILLO TECHNICAL COLLEGE

The Brewing Industry

The Brewing Industry

A Study in Industrial
Organisation and Public Policy

K.H. Hawkins

Lecturer in Industrial Relations,
Management Centre, University of Bradford

C.L. Pass

Lecturer in Industrial Economics,
Management Centre, University of Bradford

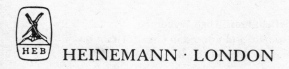

HEINEMANN · LONDON

Heinemann Educational Books Ltd
22 Bedford Square, London WC1B 3HH

LONDON EDINBURGH MELBOURNE AUCKLAND
HONG KONG SINGAPORE KUALA LUMPUR NEW DEHLI
IBADAN LUSAKA NAIROBI JOHANESBURG
EXETER (NH) KINGSTON PORT OF SPAIN

ISBN 0 435 84399 0 (Cased)
       0 435 84400 8 (Limp)

Typeset by The Castlefield Press, High Wycombe
in 10/12 pt Journal Roman, and printed in Great Britain by
Richard Clay (The Chaucer Press) Ltd., Bungay, Suffolk

Preface

The brewing industry has long been of interest to public policy-makers, economists and social reformers. As early as the sixteenth century social concern with the evils of drink abuse led to the establishment of a system of licensing controls and at one point the 'nationalisation' of the trade appeared a possibility. More recently, attention has been directed towards the economic conduct and performance of the industry. The National Board for Prices and Incomes (1966 and 1969), the Monopolies Commission (1969) and the Price Commission (1977) in turn have voiced criticisms of certain aspects of the industry's organisation and its use of resources.

This new study of the brewing industry looks at the evolution of the industry since the rise of commercial brewing in the nineteenth century. The factors which led to the early establishment of the tied public house system are discussed, and particular emphasis is given to the recent merger movement in the industry which has resulted in the emergence of the national brewing groups. The implications of these structural developments for competition and the 'public interest' are analysed in detail and the policy options which now confront the state, as the ultimate arbiter of the licensing laws, are presented.

The brewing industry provides a good illustration of certain aspects of applied economic analysis, in particular those relating to the balance of supply and demand, competition and concentration, vertical integration and associations between market structure, conduct and economic performance. It also provides fertile ground for examining the impact of social and public policy influences on economic processes, in particular the brewers' attempt to reconcile conventional business practices with the constraints placed upon them by a policy of restrictive licensing designed to control alcoholic abuse.

Acknowledgements

We would like to extend our thanks to Mr Burns of the Brewers' Society, for assistance in researching the book, Jo Baxter and Sylvia Ashdown for typing the manuscript, and Jayne Potter for her help in preparing the book for publication.

K. H. Hawkins
C. L. Pass
Management Centre,
University of Bradford
October 1978

Contents

List of Tables

1 Introduction

The Modern Brewing Industry: an Overview

Between the late 1940s and the early 1970s, the social and economic status of the brewing industry was transformed. In the immediate post-war period the structure and conduct of the industry were not very different from what they had been thirty years earlier. The industry was still fragmented and localised in its structure, with national firms accounting for only one quarter of total output. Most firms were still dominated by family interests and this had a pervasive effect on the conduct of the industry. As Vaizey observed, in these old-established family firms 'traditional patterns and loyalties' limited the seizing of profit opportunities and restrained commercial 'pushfulness'.[1]

These patterns of behaviour were strongly reinforced by the framework of restrictive licensing and the overt, though declining, hostility towards the liquor trade which still existed in certain quarters. The need to conduct their business in a socially-responsible manner frequently made it difficult for the brewers to conform to the conventional norms of commercial behaviour. In Seldon's words:

> Brewing is not the only industry that takes a long and wide view of its business decisions but it exhibits this broader view perhaps more plainly than do other industries. Unprofitable houses may be kept year after year; beers are not always discontinued when the demand for them falls below the margin at which revenue covers costs; tenants who have long since seen their best days are sometimes kept well into old age . . .. In other words, profits have sometimes been put second to prestige, or popularity, or, not least, pride: a son who inherits a business will wish to pass it on undiminished.[2]

Finally, the industry was still narrow in scope. Few firms had interests outside brewing and retailing beer; the manufacture of soft drinks was a minority interest, and the wine and spirit trade was still largely in the hands of independent suppliers. Retailing itself was defined overwhelmingly in terms of tied trade. The ownership of licensed houses was seen as proper and reputable; selling beer to the free trade was more 'commercial', risky and therefore questionable. The experiences of the inter-war period produced a general expectation, both inside and outside the industry, that the demand for beer would continue to decline.

Yet the tied house system gave almost every firm a degree of market security so that even in the worst years of the inter-war depression there were no forced closures. As Vaizey pointed out, an oligopolistic situation existed in which secure profits were made.[3]

But while profits were secure, the overall return on capital was low. The industry's main asset — its licensed estate — may have been managed in a way that was socially responsible, but hard economic realities could not be ignored indefinitely. As long as the industry appeared locked into a situation of long-term decline and low returns, there was no obvious incentive for new sources of enterprise to seek entry into the industry. During the second half of the 1950s, however, beer consumption stopped falling and then began to show a modest annual increase. The rapid spread of television ownership, contrary to popular expectations, did not succeed in 'killing' the public house. The long process of regional concentration within the industry continued and, freed from post-war building restrictions, the brewers began the long task of renovating and improving their licensed houses after years of enforced neglect. It was at this point, however, that outsiders began to realise the potential which lay within the industry for future development. The take-over bid for Watney Mann by Sears Holdings was based on the discrepancy between the existing and alternative-use values of licensed property. The activities of E. P. Taylor and his group of companies underlined the logic of achieving comprehensive national coverage in order to exploit and develop the emerging national market. The development of keg beer reinforced the case for national expansion by making the distribution of draught beer in bulk over long distances commercially feasible. Thus the merger boom between 1959 and 1962 was motivated by both offensive and defensive pressures. The threat of being acquired by an unwelcome bidder induced many firms to arrange for their own acquisition by an 'acceptable' neighbour. Even in this period of unprecedentedly rapid concentration, therefore, certain traditions were preserved and contested bids were rare. Nevertheless, as these defensive alliances increased in number and size, so the national groups began to emerge and the advantages of national coverage became increasingly apparent.

The growth of a national market for beer had been foreshadowed in the success which the larger groups had had during the immediate post-war period in promoting a small number of branded bottled beers. This trend in consumer taste was accelerated by the development of keg bitter and lager. Thus, while the consumption of traditional cask beer declined, there was an overall swing in taste away from bottled beer and towards keg and 'pressurised' draught beer. Eventually, in the early 1970s, there was an adverse reaction to these trends from a minority of articulate consumers, which may have given some psychological impetus to those independent firms who still relied largely on cask beer. Nevertheless the overall trend in consumer tastes was, and remains, unambiguously in favour of national and well-known regional brands of 'pressurised' beers and, increasingly, lager. The importance of achieving national coverage and of marketing national and well-known regional brands was reinforced by the growing significance of the free trade. From 1961 onwards, a more liberal framework of licensing facilitated a sustained expansion in the number of off-licences, while other types of on-licences (except public houses) also continued to grow. The free trade had long been dominated by those brewers who marketed well-known brands of bottled beer and the development of keg beer and lager enabled the national brewers to extend their sales into this expanding sector of the market.

As in the last quarter of the nineteenth century, the market environment combined with the prevailing framework of licensing to produce major changes in the conduct of the industry. In the late Victorian era, the conjunction of declining demand and restrictive licensing emphasised the logic of vertical integration, and the ownership of retail outlets became the pre-condition of survival. During the 1960s, by contrast, consumption was set on a firm upward trend while the number of retail outlets was steadily increasing. A more liberal approach to licensing meant that the retail trade became open — for the first time in nearly a century — to the small entrepreneur. The barriers against entry into brewing itself, however, remained formidable. The expansion of the free trade, therefore, compelled the brewers as a whole to abandon their traditional reluctance to compete in this sector of the market. Price competition was a major force in the free trade and this tended to favour the national and major regional brewers who were in a better position than small firms to offer loan facilities, attractive discounts on bulk purchases and, of course, well-known brands. The possibilities for growth in the free trade, however, meant that no brewer could afford to ignore this sector of the market. Consequently, the industry as a whole — and particularly the national firms — became less and less dependent on sales of beer through their own tied outlets. In other words, for the national brewers at least, vertical integration — defined as the ownership of retail outlets or the tied house system — began to lose some of its traditional significance. One important symptom of this trend was the development of a more rigorous, 'commercial' approach to the management of licensed property. From the early 1960s onwards tied houses were closed voluntarily and on a scale which would have been impossible only ten years earlier and inconceivable to the previous generation of brewers. Rationalisation of tied estates was, however, accompanied by investment in improving the amenities of licensed houses on an unprecedented scale. The growing realisation within the industry that the public house was competing within a wider and increasingly sophisticated leisure market meant not only that the standard ameties had to be improved but also that a wider range of them had to be provided. Tenant licensees also had to be given more incentive to exploit these opportunities. As a result, the traditional approach to tied house rents was abandoned. The brewing industry's growing significance within the leisure market was finally sealed in the early 1970s by the appearance of new competitors through 'take-over' entry.

Anticipating at least some of the changes which were about to overtake the industry, from the vantage point of the early 1950s Seldon warned that the brewers needed 'skill and patience to adapt the practices and attitudes of decades to the harsh economic realities of today without impairing social and public approval'.[4] The increasing popularity of the public house during the 1960s and 1970s suggests that the brewers have in large measure succeeded in reconciling these potentially conflicting pressures. They have proved that social responsibility and economic efficiency are not incompatible. The changes in the structure and conduct of the industry noted above, however, have taken place in a climate of opinion which is increasingly aware of the potential threat to social welfare posed by concentrated market power. Vertical integration was tolerated so long as the horizontal structure of the brewing industry remained relatively fragmented. The emergence of the national groups, however, brought a rapid concentration of horizontal market power which, when added to the traditional presence of vertical integration, aroused the suspicion of welfare-minded economists. Unfortunately, much of the criticism which has been directed at the industry since the mid-1960s has failed to distinguish between the effects of vertical integration as such and the consequences of horizontal market power.

In view of the declining importance of the tied house system within the retail liquor market as a whole, it may seem odd that it still continues to arouse so much hostility. A cynical observer might maintain that while competition policy-enforcers can do nothing to break down the concentration of horizontal market power within the industry, they could nevertheless recommend that steps be taken to destroy the brewers' hold on one section of the on-licensed trade. A more persuasive explanation, however, lies in the growing normative influence of price competition over public policy makers. In an age when State regulation of wage and price determination is regarded as a political necessity, there are strong and obvious pressures on governments and their agencies to ensure that price competition is a reality, particularly in those markets which supply goods to the majority of the population. In the case of the brewing industry, the rapid expansion of the take-home trade — a sector of the market in which price competition is undoubtedly a major influence — has led outside investigators to the conclusion that the weakness of price competition in the on-licensed trade is the direct result of vertical integration. This conclusion is mistaken. One major theme of this study is to show that, while the social role and status of the public house have undergone several important changes over the past century, the intrinsic nature of beer retailing itself has remained largely constant. As long as the public house remains a predominantly social institution, the main focus of competitive behaviour must continue to be in the provision of amenities, which does not, of course, exclude price flexibility. The competitive provision of amenities would occupy the same strategic role even if brewer ownership of licensed houses was to be abolished. What brewer ownership has achieved, as most outside investigators have admitted, is the provision of an increasingly wider range of higher quality amenities than would otherwise have been possible. And, contrary to the claims of some investigators, this has been achieved — at least in recent years — without any conspicuous misallocation of resources.

Competition Theory, Public Policy and the Brewing Industry

The performance of firms and markets is conventionally evaluated in terms of the contribution that they make to the enhancement of general economic welfare. Competition in the market place is seen as a particularly important force in ensuring that the pursuit of the private interests of suppliers of products and services is compatible with an economic performance that is also social optimal. In this section we set the scene for a more detailed analysis of the brewing industry's conduct and performance by looking at the nature and significance of 'competition' as founded in economic theory and public policy.

'Competition' as a behavioural process refers to the active rivalry of firms for customers. It consists of a combination of initiatory actions by a firm and a complex of responses from that firm's rivals. In this process of active market rivalry, the entrepreneur has at least four parameters of action at his disposal – selling price, physical product differentiation, selling efforts and product innovation. 'Market power' is defined as the ability of a seller to determine within limits the supply terms of his offering to buyers without immediate encroachment by competitors. According to Clark: 'It is the ability of the firm to behave persistently in a manner different from the behaviour that a competitive market would enforce on a firm facing otherwise similar cost and demand conditions.'[5] The problem is, of course, that almost all industries exhibit some degree of market power. In practice, therefore, public policy, both in the UK and elsewhere, tends to focus not only on the possession of market power as such, but more especially on the way in which this power is exercised.[6]

Investigations into the possession and use of market power in a given industry conventionally begin by analysing the market structure. The most important structural elements are, firstly, the degree of seller and buyer concentration; secondly, the degree of product differentiation among competing offerings; and thirdly, the conditions of entry into the market. If, at one extreme, a market is atomistically organised with each firm contributing only a fraction of total supply and if product differentiation is low and entry easy, the individual firm will have little or no discretionary power. If, at the other extreme, monopoly conditions apply and entry is blocked, one firm will be able to exercise total control over the market, subject to competition from substitute products. Between these polar extremes, however, lie an immense number of variable blends of competition and discretionary market power. In Clark's words:

> The specific character of competition in any given case depends on a surprisingly large number of conditions – so many, in fact, that the number of mathematically possible combinations runs into the hundreds of thousands – and suggests the possibility that every industry may be in some significant respect different from every other, or from itself at some other stage of development.[7]

Most markets are in fact oligopolistic and, as such, are characterised by high levels of seller concentration and difficult entry. Yet this kind of structural data may in itself throw little light on the nature of competition within a given market. As the level of seller concentration in a market increases, it is not always possible to state unambiguously that there has been a lessening of competition. Competition among the few may be just as vigorous as competition among the many, although the character of the competitive process may be different with, for example, oligopolists preferring to rely on product differentiation rather than price rivalry. The characteristic which is held to be common to all oligopolistic markets is that sellers are dependent on each other's decisions. Yet this mutual dependency may be expressed in different ways. At one extreme firms may simply recognise that competitive initiatives are likely to be matched by similar responses from their rivals. At the other extreme, firms may seek to exercise collective market power through tacit or overt collusion.

The significance of market structure lies not only in its relevance to the origins of market power, but also in its implications for the conduct and performance of a given industry. Assuming that firms seek to maximise their profits and that they possess full information about their rivals and their market, conventional market theory attempts to explain and predict differences in market performance when structural parameters are altered. Analysed in terms of 'comparative statics', competitive markets are shown to yield performance results superior to those characterised by monopoly elements.[8] In the real world, however, almost all markets are oligopolistic, and no general theory for this type of market yet exists. This deficiency has, of course, created a problem for public policy-makers. In McKie's words: 'Public policy does not and should not require perfect competition in most markets, but it should seek to establish or encourage market patterns in which adequate performance is compelled by market structure.[9] The requirements of competition policy have led to the adoption by public bodies, both in the UK and the USA, of the concept of 'workable' or 'effective' competition. As Allen has pointed out, workable competition

> is concerned with the factors that stimulate economic rivalry and is therefore a dynamic concept. It tries to judge forms of industrial organisation and the policies of firms by reference to the extent to which they promote this rivalry. It recognises that monopoly elements are inevitably present in most market situations and it seeks ways in which these can be made compatible with active competitive behaviour. The main condition for the existence of workable competition is that both buyers and sellers should have before them 'an adequate number of alternative courses of action'. This concept is far from precise and leaves the determination of what is adequate to be decided in particular cases.[10]

What kind of market structure is likely to promote effective competition? In Clark's view, favourable conditions '. . . include a substantial number of firms small enough, relative to the whole structure in which they compete, to have strong competitive incentives (though there is no need for atomistic smallness) and economically strong enough to make their competitive pressure count'.[11] He thus takes into account the influence of the number of firms in a market and is also aware that firms must be large enough to be able to exploit economies of scale. But if the objective of workable competition is to encourage technical progress and efficiency on the one hand, while ensuring supplies to markets at prices approximating to minimum costs on the other, is it not at least possible that the same objective may be achieved by increasing concentration? It was Schumpeter's view that monopoly power is necessary in order to justify substantial expenditure on research and development.[12] In addition, Williamson has argued that 'a merger which yields non-trivial real economies must produce substantial market power and result in relatively large price increases for the net allocative (i.e. welfare) effects to be negative' or, in other words, that there is at least a strong *a priori* likelihood that concentration which produced real economies of scale could result in lower prices than competition among many smaller firms.[13] It must also be recognised, however, that 'organisational slack' tends to be reduced when inter-firm competition is strong.[14] Support for the argument that competitive pressure is a powerful stimulus to the reduction of costs, even within a given technology, has been provided by Leibenstein, who terms the efficiency stimulus from this source 'X-efficiency'.[15] Thus, both economies of scale and a competitive environment may exert downward pressure on costs, but it is only the latter which can ensure that such benefits are passed on to the consumer in that form which results, in Clark's terms, in the profits of the bulk of firms approximating to 'the minimum necessary supply price of capital and enterprise'. Thus, whilst recognising that competing firms need to be large enough to sustain active rivalry in the long term, Clark maintains that concentration 'is not favourable to the kinds of competition that make for rapid and adequate diffusion of the benefits'.[16]

One would not expect a market structure characterised by a high degree of vertical integration to pass the test of workable competition. The distinguishing feature of vertical integration is that it enables a firm to by-pass one or more markets and to this extent reduces competition. Backward integration refers to a situation in which the firm undertakes the production of raw materials or semi-fabricated inputs which were previously supplied to it by independent producers. Forward integration occurs when a firm engages not only in the production or final assembly of a particular product but also undertakes the wholesaling and retailing operations which put that product into the hands of consumers.[17] Thus, the greater the degree of vertical integration in a given industry, the greater the opportunity there may be for the abuse of market power. More specifically, vertical integration has been attacked by exponents of workable competition on several grounds: firstly, that it may hinder the entry of new firms or limit the growth of established firms by foreclosing either market outlets or supplies of inputs; secondly, that it may enable integrated firms to apply price discrimination or 'price-squeezing' in order to neutralise competition from non-integrated firms; thirdly, that it may be a means whereby a firm can extend or maintain a dominant market position, and finally that it may transmit oligopolistic influences from one stage to others in which they are currently absent, thereby inhibiting price competition in the stage entered. In the case of the brewing industry, for example, the Monopolies Commission argued that a situation in which the brewers owned 78 per cent of full on-licensed outlets and 48 per cent of all retail outlets was unlikely to be in the public interest. Vertical integration was alleged to have hindered the entry of new producers and new products, retarded the elimination of high-cost production capacity and stifled price competition.[18]

The validity of the Monopolies Commission's case against the tied house system will be analysed in the course of this study. At this stage, however, it is necessary to ask whether public suspicion of vertical integration has any foundation in economic theory. Static theory offers no support to the argument that vertical integration is likely to result in lower output and higher prices to the final consumer, and this conclusion applies irrespective of whether one or both stages of production or distribution are monopolies or perfectly competitive. Thus, the main motive for backward or forward integration would seem to be the appropriation of the profits in the stage entered. Reductions in costs cannot be generally predicted, but may apply in particular cases.[19] The more recent managerial theories of the firm, applied in a dynamic context, tend to emphasise the importance of economies of integration associated with transactional inefficiencies in the intermediate market. They also stress the advantages of integration over contractual agreements, in so far as the integrated firm has better instruments of control (such as access to information which can be used to evaluate the performance of personnel and develop more effective reward and penalty instruments) which can be used to reduce transactional inefficiencies.[20] Whether or not the economies of integration are passed on to the consumer, however, depends on the degree of monopoly power which the integrated firms have in the final market.

To what extent, therefore, does vertical integration *per se* increase monopoly power? In the extreme case of a fully integrated industry — where one or a few manufacturers own the key sources of supply and all the channels of distribution — no entry is feasible at any level without entry at all levels. Hence any firm intending to go into such an industry requires vast amounts of capital, which tends to discourage and drastically reduce the number of prospective entrants.[21] The newcomer or small firm has to convince outside sources of capital, with no existing stake in the venture, that its proposed entry is likely to be a profitable venture. If the supply curve of capital is positively sloped and relatively inelastic, then '. . . established firms may use vertical integration strategically to increase finance requirements and thereby to discourage entry if potential entrants feel compelled . . . to adopt the prevailing structure, as they may if the industry is highly concentrated'.[22] Although there is no conclusive research to support this argument, it is an established tenet of modern economic theory that non-price competition is prevalent in oligopolistic markets, and empirical evidence underlines the significance to entry of product-differentiation barriers. On the whole oligopolists feel that more permanent advantages can be gained over rivals through non-price competition because successful product differentiation, reinforced by competition through the marketing mix (including branding, packaging, selling efforts and distribution) cannot be matched as quickly and completely as price reductions. This suggests that the weakness of price competition in an integrated market may be more attributable to the existence of horizontal market power than to vertical integration.[23] It may also be the case, however, that vertical integration does in itself raise product-differentiation barriers to entry.[24]

The alleged relationship between vertical integration and non-price competitive behaviour is particularly relevant to the welfare assumptions of workable competition. It has been argued that if competition is effective, industry is compelled to use its resources efficiently and the public as a whole will benefit in terms of the price, quality and choice of goods offered for sale.[25] In practice the encouragement of rivalry between firms has been seen primarily in terms of promoting price competition. This emphasis has if anything increased in recent years as successive governments have introduced and maintained as an integral part of their counter-inflation strategies stringent controls on prices and dividends. It is assumed that the benefits of price competition are such that it should be encouraged in all factor and product markets, particularly since there is an observed tendency for oligopolists to restrict this form of rivalry. Since vertical integration cuts out competition in supply, raises entry barriers and gives each firm a relatively secure share of the market, it can be argued that this institution must encourage non-competitive behaviour (i.e. non-price competition). Thus, in the case of the brewing industry, the Price Commission (1977) asserted that the tied house system had, by erecting almost insuperable barriers to new entrants, given the brewers a protected market within which there was little price competition and little incentive to improve efficiency. The concentration of ownership of public houses was, the Commission concluded '. . . unlikely to be in the interests of the consumer' and had 'certainly not brought lower prices'.[26] It is, however, quite legitimate to question the assumption that competitive behaviour within the tied public house trade must be evaluated according to exactly the same criteria as would be applied to any other section of the retail trade. For it is at least arguable that until quite recently the conduct of the liquor trade in general and of public houses in particular has been evaluated within a normative framework totally different from that of workable competition. The system of liquor licensing has imposed certain normative standards on brewers and licensees alike, and these in turn reflect the wider expectations of society. These standards have gradually changed as society itself has changed, yet the fundamental problem of reconciling economic criteria and social values remains.

The significance of social norms and expectations raises a further problem with obvious implications for the concept of workable competition, namely that of evaluating the factors which determine the business policies of individual firms. Theorists have tended to assume that each firm sets out with the objective of maximising profits. Empirical research, however, throws considerable doubt on this assumption. The formal study of business policy has emphasised that firms differ by size, organisation, form of control and product-market scope, and that these characteristics can be used to place a given firm at a particular stage in 'corporate development'. Firms in different stages of corporate development will tend to pursue different business strategies.[27] If this is so, then even if firms in the same market did have the same objective, namely profit maximisation, there would be no guarantee that their methods of achieving this objective and consequently their market behaviour would also be the same. Their interpretation of 'maximum profits' would differ, as indeed would the time horizons within which this objective had to be achieved. In terms of Clark's formulation of effective competition, this would mean that initiatory moves by some firms might not be perceived as a strong enough threat by other firms in the same market to warrant a defensive response. In other words, because firms are likely to be at different stages of corporate development, it is likely that they will react differently to a particular initiatory move. Bearing in mind that Clark sees initiatory moves and defensive responses extending over a long period, it might well be difficult to judge at any given moment in time whether or not competition within a particular market was effective.

It is reasonable to suggest, therefore, that definitions of workable competition which concentrate almost exclusively on the structural characteristics of markets may well mislead the makers of public policy. In structural terms, workable competition requires that there be a sufficient number of firms in a market, each of sufficient size to ensure that a series of initiatory moves and defensive responses will occur and continue into the long term. These, in turn, will ensure that most firms in the market do not gain more than a minimum level of profits sufficient to enable them to take advantage of technical developments and continue to develop and introduce new products and production techniques. This kind of generalisation, however, begs a number of obvious questions. What is a 'sufficient' number of firms? How concentrated must a market become before the firms operating in it acquire 'excessive' market power? How are we to judge whether or not the performance of these firms is 'efficient'? The conventional response has taken the form of a 'shopping list' of performance standards or norms (covering profits, costs, pricing behaviour and barriers to entry) which are assumed to be compatible with workable competition. It has been pointed out, however, that these norms have only limited significance in so far as they are based on comparisons with other similar industries. Consequently the need for public intervention is measured primarily according to how far the performance norms of a given industry differ from those of the industries with which it has been compared. It has also been argued that since this approach has no theoretical basis, it provides no way of evaluating the weight to be given to individual norms, resolving conflicts between norms, or measuring the extent to which norms are interdependent. Finally, it has been pointed out that, in practice, there are immense difficulties involved in obtaining conclusive empirical evidence about the extent to which performance standards are actually achieved by a firm or a group of firms.[28]

The conventional argument that market structure largely determines conduct and peformance has emerged in successive investigations of the brewing industry over the past few years. The most recent of these investigations, for example, concluded that 'the way this trade is organised and run has a profound effect on prices and profits'.[29] Vertical integration has, it is alleged, erected high barriers to entry and given the brewers a protected market in which there is no incentive to compete through price. The Monopolies Commission apparently believed, however, that vertical integration is, and always has been, maintained and justified by restrictive licensing. The implications for public policy are self-evident. If restrictive licensing is abolished, or at least seriously weakened, the need for the brewers to own retail outlets will also be removed. This study will argue, however, that the origins of vertical integration may be found in the nature of beer retailing and in the changing demand for beer rather than in restrictive licensing. To this extent the scope for increasing competition through manipulating the framework of licensing may be less than is commonly supposed. But, more fundamentally, the argument that structure determines conduct and performance will be critically examined in this study. This will require a detailed analysis of all the other factors that have shaped the business policies pursued by brewery companies, particularly the requirements of social responsibility. Vaizey, for example, has suggested 'the constant preoccupation of brewers with the State and politics may have limited their commercial enterprise'.[30] Is this conclusion justified? How, in fact, has the brewing industry attempted to reconcile the need for economic efficiency with the obligations of social responsibility? Once this question has been answered, it may be possible to suggest that the existing market structure has been shaped, at least in part, by the conduct and performance of the industry in the past.

For this reason the relationship between structure, conduct and performance has been presented in this study within its dynamic historical framework. It is hoped that by means of this approach the reader will obtain a clearer impression of the way in which the market structure has responded to changes in business policy, which in turn have their origins in the interaction of social, economic and political pressures. Particular attention will be paid to the following questions: (i) Why did the brewers begin to buy public houses when they did? (ii) What were the effects of this development on the conduct and performance of the industry? (iii) What other factors have influenced business policy? (iv) Is there anything that public policy could usefully do in order to make competition within the industry more effective while simultaneously avoiding any undesirable social consequences?

2 Background to the Modern Industry

The Rise of Commercial Brewing

The brewing process itself has changed very little over the centuries. Water is infused with malt in a mash tun under conditions favouring the conversion of starch into fermentable sugars; the extract is boiled with hops to achieve biochemical and biological stability; the liquid is then cooled and yeast is added; in the subsequent fermentation stage the yeast assimilates the sugars dissolved from the malt and turns them into alcohol. The beer is then allowed to mature for periods which depend upon its composition and its markets. The basic brewing process is illustrated in Figure 1.

Down the years the rural structure of society and the simplicity of the brewing process confined the industry to its original craft tradition, the trade being characterised by innumerable semi-domestic publican brewers who produced beer either for their own consumption or for sale on their own premises.

In the nineteenth century, however, the industrialisation movement brought with it new urban markets and this, together with the application of science and technology to the traditional 'brewers art' served to raise the optimal scale of brewing operations and led to the rise of 'commercial' brewing. As large towns grew, so did the possibility of large breweries, because the commercial brewers required large populations to consume their outputs and their delivery area was limited by transport costs. London, where commercial brewing began in the early years of the eighteenth century, was the most important centre. By 1800 the breweries of such firms as Whitbread, and Barclay Perkins were producing 100,000 to 200,000 barrels a year. In the provinces large-scale brewing developed in the main industrial centres, especially in the Burton area where Bass and Allsopp came to dominate the trade. The largest brewer of them all was Arthur Guinness, which had a virtual monopoly of the trade in Ireland and whose distinctive stout was to become famous throughout England with the coming of the railway age.

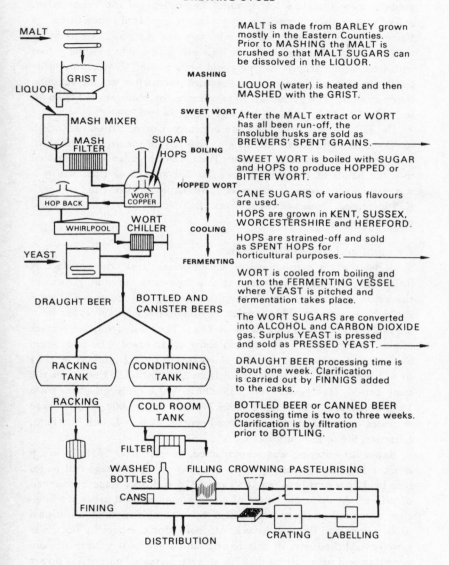

IND COOPE LTD.
BREWING CYCLE

MALT

GRIST

LIQUOR

MASH MIXER

MASH FILTER

SUGAR

HOPS

WORT COPPER

HOP BACK

WHIRLPOOL

WORT CHILLER

YEAST

DRAUGHT BEER

BOTTLED AND CANISTER BEERS

RACKING TANK

RACKING

CONDITIONING TANK

COLD ROOM TANK

FILTER

FINING

WASHED BOTTLES

CANS

FILLING CROWNING PASTEURISING

CRATING LABELLING

DISTRIBUTION

MASHING

SWEET WORT

BOILING

HOPPED WORT

COOLING

FERMENTING

MALT is made from BARLEY grown mostly in the Eastern Counties. Prior to MASHING the MALT is crushed so that MALT SUGARS can be dissolved in the LIQUOR.

LIQUOR (water) is heated and then MASHED with the GRIST.

After the MALT extract or WORT has all been run-off, the insoluble husks are sold as BREWERS' SPENT GRAINS.

SWEET WORT is boiled with SUGAR and HOPS to produce HOPPED or BITTER WORT.

CANE SUGARS of various flavours are used.

HOPS are grown in KENT, SUSSEX, WORCESTERSHIRE and HEREFORD.

HOPS are strained-off and sold as SPENT HOPS for horticultural purposes.

WORT is cooled from boiling and run to the FERMENTING VESSEL where YEAST is pitched and fermentation takes place.

The WORT SUGARS are converted into ALCOHOL and CARBON DIOXIDE gas. Surplus YEAST is pressed and sold as PRESSED YEAST.

DRAUGHT BEER processing time is about one week. Clarification is carried out by FINNIGS added to the casks.

BOTTLED BEER or CANNED BEER processing time is two to three weeks. Clarification is by filtration prior to BOTTLING.

Figure 1.

Before the railway age markets necessarily remained fragmented and so for many years the small publican-brewer managed to co-exist alongside his larger commercial rivals. From the 1830s onwards, however, the publican-brewer rapidly lost ground. The linking of the major urban areas by the railway network exposed him to increased competition. As Vaizey noted: 'His methods were archaic and his product was often inferior. Any commercial brewer was eventually able to supply him with beer more cheaply than he could brew himself'.[1] More and more publicans stopped brewing and confined themselves to the retailing function alone. The percentage of beer brewed by publicans fell from 40 in 1841-45 to 10 in 1886-90 and was negligible by 1914.[2]

The railway revolution and the concurrent urbanisation of English society thus transformed the brewing industry in the second and third quarters of the nineteenth century. The bulk of beer production passed into the hands of commercial brewers. The growth of a national railway network broadened the brewers' marketing horizons and competition increased. Demand expanded and the industry moved into a period of growth and prosperity.

Demand and the Retail Market

Since beer was a predominantly working-class drink, the key factors influencing the level of demand at this time were the rapid growth in the urban working-class population, their rising real incomes and their social circumstances. The population of England and Wales rose from 8.8 millions in 1801 to 26 millions in 1881. The most significant feature of this growth was that it was essentially urban-based. The population of Greater London, for example, increased from 2.2 millions in 1841 to 4.7 millions in 1881; Liverpool from 286,000 to 553,000 over the same period; Manchester from 235,000 to 462,000; Birmingham from 183,000 to 437,000; Glasgow from 275,000 to 587,000. Similar large increases occurred in other industrial centres such as Leeds, Sheffield, Leicester, Stoke and Edinburgh.

Rapid urbanisation was accompanied, at least after 1850, by a significant increase in working class spending power. Average real wages rose by 37 per cent between 1850 and 1876 as money wages rose ahead of prices.[3] At this time habits of consumption in most urban working-class communities were determined by a combination of traditional social norms and limited choices. Alcoholic drink, especially beer, was a well-established part of this narrow and traditional pattern of consumption and up to the mid-1870s at least, increased purchasing power tended to go in this direction. The general squalor of the urban environment, together with the lack of alternative recreational opportunities, induced most working men to spend their leisure time in the nearest public house.[4]

The combined effect of these factors served to bring about a substantial increase in beer output and consumption. The average annual output of beer rose from 14.6 million barrels in 1830-35 to 31 million barrels in 1875-79, while *per capita* consumption of beer increased from 21.7 gallons to 33.2 gallons over the same period (Table 2.1).

Table 2.1. Beer output, consumption and real wages, 1850-1914

Year	Beer output million barrels	Per head (gallons)	Average real wages (1850 = 100)
1850-54	16.13	22.5	101.2
1855-59	17.22	22.0	96.2
1860-64	19.93	24.7	105.8
1865-69	24.28	28.8	111.6
1870-74	27.58	31.1	127.4
1875-79	30.97	33.2	132.0
1880-84	28.50	29.1	137.2
1885-89	28.70	28.3	149.4
1890-94	31.50	29.7	164-0
1895-99	34.60	31.2	176.4
1900-04	35.20	30.2	175.2
1905-09	33.20	27.3	173.0
1910-14	34.10	26.9	171.2

Source: G. B. Wilson, *Alcohol and the Nation*, Nicholson and Watson, 1940; B. R. Mitchell and P. Deane, *Abstracts of British Historical Statistics*, Cambridge University Press, 1962.

The mid-Victorian boom in beer consumption was also facilitated in part by the official policy of 'free' licensing which prevailed in 1830-69. The licensing of establishments selling beer had been first introduced in 1552, powers being vested in local justices of the peace.[5] Down to 1660 strict control over the number of licences was exercised. There then followed a period of laxness which went virtually unchecked down to 1787. In that year, however, following growing concern over the large and increasing number of beer and ale-houses and the 'unruly and rowdy' behaviour of their clientele, a new Act empowered the justices to reduce the number of licences in areas of superfluity and to exercise firmer control of those that remained.[6] This policy of restriction and regulation, while good for the social order, was considered in some quarters to have produced harmful economic side-effects. In 1817 a Select Committee of the House of Commons, concerned at the practice of the London brewers of 'tying' public houses to exclusive dealing arrangements, considered that the trade was too closed and recommended a more liberal approach to licensing. Gradually, benches relaxed their attitudes towards the granting of new licences until the movement finally culminated in 1830 in two measures designed to create 'free trade' in beer. The first was the budget of that year, which removed the tax on beer; the second was the Beer Act under which any ratepayer wishing to sell beer on his own premises could do so without having to obtain a justices' license. The objective was to create a new class of drinking establishment outside the control of both the magistrates and the commercial brewers. Within 10 years of this Act, nearly 40,000 new 'beerhouses' had been established. Over the period of the life of the Act (1830-69) the number of beerhouses rose to 46,135 (annual average, 1865-69), while the number of licensed public houses increased from an average of 52,900 (1830-34) to 68,300 (1865-69).[7]

Paradoxically, however, the main economic effect of 'free' licensing was to further strengthen the hand of the commercial brewers. In London itself relatively few beerhouses were established (about 1,100) and their proprietors found themselves in exactly the same state of dependence on the commercial brewers in the city as established publicans. In the industrial towns, this Act enabled the retail trade to respond to the opportunities offered by growing urbanisation, but again it was usually the commercial brewer who was in the best position to exploit these opportunities.

Most public houses in London were leasehold and as the value of property was considerably higher there than elsewhere, and rising rapidly, it had long been customary for outgoing tenants to ask their successors for a 'goodwill' payment on the lease. The size of the payment demanded induced most incoming tenants to obtain a loan from the brewer or brewers who customarily supplied the house.[8] These loans were given in return for an undertaking by the tenant to deal exclusively with the brewer concerned in respect of his beer supplies. By the late eighteenth century the 'loan-tie' was widespread in London, being regarded by brewer and tenant alike as a logical and legitimate business arrangement. Although the London brewers did acquire some public house leases on their own behalf during the first three-quarters of the nineteenth century, the loan-tie which they had over an otherwise independent leaseholder remained far more significant.[9]

In the provinces, the situation was less clear cut. Contemporaries who were sympathetic to the brewing trade tended, when commenting on the growth of the tied house system during the last quarter of the century, to put the blame on the re-establishment of restrictive licensing in 1869 and suggested that up to then the country brewers had no reason to purchase licensed houses. In the absence of adequate statistics, it is difficult to arrive at any firm conclusions about the extent of the tie outside London. There is some evidence to suggest that the tie was relatively common in the industrial towns and seaports and rare in the remoter rural areas.[10] As in London though, the tie took the form principally of a loan arrangement with an independent victualler rather than direct ownership of the premises. It seems unlikely, however, because of the rapid growth of the market, that the commercial brewers at this time relied extensively on supplying tied outlets. As the national railway network was completed, the possibilities of exploiting a wider market became increasingly evident to many brewers. Interestingly, it was the major Burton brewers who took the lead in this field and established their commercial reputations in the national market which the railway system opened up in the three decades after 1840.

Competition and the Burton Brewers

In order to understand the reasons for the rapid growth of the Burton trade between the 1840s and the 1870s, it is necessary to consider the changing character of competition in the brewing industry at this time. In the mid-Victorian era competition between commercial brewers revolved around the flavour, strength and reliability of their brews. Regional and local tastes were also of crucial importance. In London the main beer was 'porter', a strong heavy brew. The growth of porter brewing in the eighteenth century had had profound effects on the organisation of the London trade. For a variety of technical reasons porter, unlike traditional ale, could be brewed in very large quantities.[11] Thus, the rise of porter brewing led to a remarkable concentration of output in the hands of about a dozen large commercial brewers, most notably Whitbread, Barclay Perkins, Truman Hanbury Buxton, Meux, Reid, Combe Delafield, Calvert and Hoare. These brewers derived substantial cost and quality advantages from the scale of their operations. This factor, combined with the large amounts of capital needed to finance their activities, including the provision of loans to publicans, effectively deterred most would-be entrants to the London porter trade. The smaller London brewers, such as Charrington, tended to establish themselves in outlying villages, from which they could exploit that section of the trade with which, because of transport difficulties, the main London brewers did not usually concern themselves. This was the private family trade. The staple product of the family trade was 'table' beer, a lower gravity, lighter beer than porter, which carried less excise duty and was suitable for consumption with food.[12] Publican brewing ceased to be a significant factor in London in the course of the eighteenth century, and by 1830 the commercial brewers (115 in number) were responsible for about 95 per cent of beer production in the Capital.

Price competition in the conventional sense was relatively insignificant between the great porter brewers, and retail prices were generally stable. As Mathias noted,

> Competition through changing the retail price of beer in the conditions of the age had its difficulties. The public liked a traditional price: the trade was predominantly free. London Porter as brewed by the great brewers was virtually a 'standard good'. none was branded and aggressive advertisement was unknown. Price competition immediately ran up against the problem of changes in quality, which tended always to make the brewers compete in quantity rather than price under stable conditions of trade.[13]

Similarly, the Burton brewers, whose primary brew was pale ale, were concerned almost exclusively with the quality of their beers and believed that their customers would be more receptive to an increase in price than a decline in quality.

No market is entirely static for long. In London the public were beginning to develop a taste for ales. Thus, in 1833 it was noted that Barclay Perkins 'and other great houses, finding that there is a decrease in the consumption of porter and an increase in the consumption of ale, have gone into the ale trade; nearly all the *new* trade is composed of mild ale'.[14] Already, some 2,000 barrels of *Scotch Ale* (brewed by Youngers in Edinburgh) was being sold weekly in London: 'there is hardly a beerhouse but what takes in *Scotch Ale*, in addition to the brewers' ale . . . there is also ale brought from almost every county in England, and a vast quantity of stout from Dublin'.[15] The new competitive stimulus which 'imported' beers had introduced into the London market, then still the largest single market in the UK (accounting for between 20-25 per cent of total UK beer sales) was further heightened from 1840 onwards with the completion of a railway link between London and Burton. Burton pale ale was to make a remarkable impact, not only in the London trade but also in most other major consuming centres. The brew combined strength and flavour with a light, clear and sparkling appearance, in contrast to heavy porter. Despite being produced in large quantities it was still a relatively expensive product, but, as noted, good product attributes counted for more than price with a large section of the consuming public. Additionally, the Burton brewers were the first to pioneer the use of trade marks to underpin mass-marketing appeal — Bass's red triangle and Allsopp's red hand, for example, — and the use of agencies to develop sales in the 'free trade'.

The spectacular success of the leading Burton brewers in penetrating the London market and the provincial trade can be guaged from the following figures. Bass's annual average output increased from 11,300 barrels in the period 1830-34 to 957,500 in the period 1875-79. The rising demand for the company's beer necessitated the construction of two additional breweries between 1850 and 1865. By 1876 Bass's output had overtaken that of all the major London brewers, the biggest of which by this time was Truman, Hanbury Buxton with an annual output of around 600,000 barrels. Only Arthur Guinness of Dublin had a larger output than Bass. The expansion of Allsopp was hardly less impressive, with the company achieving a peak output of 900,000 barrels in 1876.

The most significant point, however, is that the tremendous growth of Bass and Allsopp between 1840 and 1875 was achieved without the assistance of tied trade. Towards the end of the period Bass at least had begun to compete in the business of advancing loans to publicans, mainly in Liverpool and London, but this was not an important element in the firm's initial growth.[16] The key factor in both cases was the quality and consistency of their beers, backed by advertising and the use of trade marks. Both relied initially on a national network of independent wholesale bottling firms who acted as their agents for the retail trade in the major urban centres. Later, as the country brewers became increasingly important, they supplemented this distribution network with agencies held by appropriate local brewers, who then sold Burton beer through their own outlets.

The great success of Bass and Allsopp led to a rapid expansion of the brewing trade at Burton. In 1837 there were 11 brewers in Burton, using a total of 75,000 bushels of malt; by 1886 there were 31 brewers in the town, using 5.8 million bushels of malt. This growth in activity was partly due to the entry of small entrepreneurs into the Burton trade. Some of these newcomers, for example, Thomas Salt, were maltsters who supplied the established concerns in Burton prior to becoming brewers themselves.[17] Burton's expansion was also aided by the arrival of several brewery firms who already operated in other areas of the country. These included, for example Peter Walker from Warrington and, significantly, the London brewers, Ind Coope, who opened a Burton branch in 1856, Charrington (1872), and Mann, Crossman and Paulin (1872), but most of the brewers who set up businesses in Burton remained small by comparison with Bass and Allsopp.

While the railway system played a vital role in the expansion of the Burton brewers, it also opened up new possibilities for other enterprising country brewers. By the 1870s even small provincial firms like John Smith of Tadcaster, Joshua Tetley of Leeds and Showell of Birmingham were sending their beer by rail to London, Manchester and other large urban markets, where they competed for publicans' custom with the Burton and Edinburgh brewers.[18] This in itself indicates that the retail trade was still relatively open and, conversely, that the significance of the 'tie' was still limited. By the 1870s, however, the free trade was becoming much more competitive. Country brewers and, increasingly, the Burton brewers found themselves obliged to offer credit facilities to publicans and compete with the London brewers in the loan-tie business, and small firms lacking the resources of the larger commercial brewers, found themselves at a growing disadvantage.[19]

Organisation and Production

The growth of urban demand, allied to changes in taste and the breakdown of the traditional barriers against competition following the spread of the railway network, brought about important changes in the structure of production which favoured the commercial brewer. From the 1830s onwards, as was noted earlier, the share of publican-brewers in total output declined rapidly and after 1851 their absolute numbers also fell. Simultaneously the number of commercial brewers increased, as did both their market share and their average output.

Table 2.2 Number of commercial brewers in England and Wales, 1831-80

Year	Number	Average output (barrels)	Percentage of total output
1831	1,654	4,312	54.5
1841	2,251	3,594	60.2
1851	2,305	4,062	62.4
1861	2,294	5,267	70.5
1870	2,512	6,755	76.8
1880	2,507	8,362	84.4

Source: J. Baxter, 'The Organisation of the Brewing Industry', unpublished Phd. thesis, London University, 1945.

The number of commercial brewers in England and Wales rose from 1,654 in 1831 to 2,507 in 1880. Average output almost doubled, and the percentage of total beer output produced by the commercial brewers increased from 54 per cent of the total to 84 per cent by 1880. The growing importance of the commercial brewers can be seen most clearly in respect of the major brewing areas (outside London) or the 'collections' (Tables 2.2 and 2.3).

Table 2.3 Growth of commercial brewing in various collections, 1861-80

Collection	Year	Number of brewers	Average output	Percentage of total output of collection
Bristol	1861	32	4,103	58
	1880	21	14,501	88
Leeds	1861	22	7,627	47
	1880	28	13,191	58
Lichfield	1861	39	25,556	79
(including Burton)	1880	57	55,866	95
Manchester	1861	105	5,521	72
	1880	92	12,005	92
Norwich	1861	20	3,970	78
	1880	23	23,834	99
Sheffield	1861	45	6,261	93
	1880	50	11,918	98

Source: J. Baxter, op.cit.

Although some concern was expressed at the increasing concentration of the trade in the hands of the commercial brewers,[20] it was generally recognised that large scale operations had brought substantial benefits. As the *Brewers' Guardian*, in its review of the trade in 1884 noted:

> This steady concentration of the trade which is now going on has many advantages, amongst which is the general improvement which is taking place in the quality of beer produced, for there is no doubt that our large brewers are able to brew beer of better quality, and more economically, than their smaller competitors.[21]

Moreover, as tastes changed and the demand for brighter, less heavy beer increased, so the need for modern equipment became more pressing. A large brewery had more capital resources with which to invest in such equipment as well as up-keep more traditional items. A large brewery was also likely to have sufficient trade to justify a degree of backward integration. The fundamental problem facing the brewers was how to produce constantly uniform beers from constantly varying raw materials. Backward integration into hop marketing and malting gave the brewers a greater degree of control over the quality and price of their principal raw materials.[22] The larger commercial brewers, therefore, had certain competitive advantages over their smaller rivals, who in turn were in a better position to respond to changing market conditions than the publican brewers.

The mid-Victorian era was, however, essentially one of transition. Although the balance of competitive advantage was moving in favour of the larger commercial brewers, it was still possible for the small-scale entrepreneur to carve himself a niche. Mathias's observation on the enterprising publican brewer of the eighteenth century was still essentially valid for his early mid-Victorian successor: 'In the most modest circumstances of entry into the trade, the origins of the entrepreneur were likely to be as humble as his capital was small'.[23] The main difference between the Georgian and Victorian entrepreneur was that the latter was an almost exclusively urban phenomenon. The transition from publican brewer to commercial brewer was much easier to achieve in a growing urban market than in a relatively stagnant rural environment. In the middle decades of the century licensed publicans and beersellers such as Robert Cain in Liverpool (1852), James Hammond in Bradford (1860), William Butler in Wolverhampton (1856) and George Offiler in Derby (1877) all became commercial brewers.[24]

The fact that the industry was becoming more concentrated and yet, at the same time, remained open to the small concern was due firstly to the rapid growth of the urban market for beer, and secondly to the increase in retail outlets which licensing relaxation had brought about. The industry did not become closed to new entrants until these two conditions disappeared — which they began to do during the 1870s. During the boom years between 1850 and 1876, however, many small commercial brewers greatly increased their output and this in turn led to an upsurge in brewery construction.

To summarise, the growth of a mass urban market, reinforced by the development of a national railway system, effectively completed the organisational transformation of the brewing industry which had begun in London during the previous century. Before the 1830s only the London section of the trade had been really 'industrialised'. Outside London, and to a lesser extent Burton, the industry was still basically a cottage industry. By 1880, however, commercial brewing was the norm in all sections of the trade and in almost every geographical area. Although London continued to form an important part of the national market for beer, the best opportunities for rapid growth were increasingly to be found in the newer urban centres of the North, Midlands and South Wales. The Beer Act of 1830 enabled the retail trade to respond to these opportunities. Between 1850 and 1876 the brewers derived enormous benefits from the rapid growth of an urban working-class, whose real incomes were rising and for whom drinking was a traditional pastime.

The growth of mass urban markets and the rise of commercial brewing made the industry much more competitive than it had been formerly, while competitive pressures were intensified by the establishment of a national railway network which led to a substantial influx of 'foreign' beers into hitherto insulated local markets. Given the existence of a relatively stable and familiar price structure in the retail trade, the main thrust of competitive initiatives was directed towards promoting brews of good quality, flavour and reliability.

Overall the period was one of considerable expansion and prosperity for all brewers. Nevertheless it must be recognised that the rapid 'commercialisation' of the industry during this period depended on a combination of factors, none of which was to last. The era of 'free' licensing came to an end in 1869; the traditional importance of beer in the spending habits of working men waned with the development of other consumer industries. Demand declined and the industry found itself with a legacy of over-capacity.

The Origins and Development of the Tied Public House System

Between 1880 and 1900 the retailing end of the brewing industry underwent a fundamental transformation. Prior to 1880 some country brewers owned the retail outlets through which their beer were sold, but the vast majority relied heavily, if not exclusively, on their ability to sell their products to independent licensed publicans. Neither the London nor the Burton brewers saw any need to involve themselves directly in retailing to any great extent. They regarded themselves as brewers, not property owners. After 1880, however, the process of forward integration accelerated and by 1900 the tied house system dominated the retail market. The implications of this development for the financial structure of the industry, for its organisation and management, and for the nature of competition, were far-reaching. The tied house system also changed the public image of the brewing industry. The view that tied trade encouraged monopolistic practices and was therefore inimical to the public interest became widespread during the 1890s and has continued down to the present day.

Originally, as we have noted, the establishment of commercial brewing was essentially a process of vertical disintegration between production and retailing as the small publican-brewer was replaced.[25]

Publicans found it increasingly more economical to buy beer from the commercial brewers than to produce it themselves. This development was however succeeded by commercial brewers' attempts to exercise some control over the retailing of their beers. In the early days of commercial brewing this was due almost entirely to technical reasons. As Vaizey noted:

> Beer was perishable and had to be handled carefully because bad handling and slow turnover could ruin the reputation of the product. Public houses with small sales could not economically stock the supplies of more than one brewer if the beer was to be sold in good condition. Above all, draught beer, because it was unbranded, was a product on which reputations could easily be lost through misrepresentation. The relative security of sale in exclusive outlets enabled the brewer to estimate demand more closely and so avoid the waste of overbrewing his perishable product.[26]

The publican, too, benefited from exclusive dealing arrangements, particularly in regard to his capital requirements which the brewer met by way of a loan advance. At this time the loan-tie arrangement rather than direct ownership governed brewer-publican relationships.

Restrictive licensing also played its part in the initial development of loan-ties. As the Webbs observed:

> When the Justices made it a practice, before granting a licence, to require that the applicant should show that he occupied premises suitable for business, they essentially passed into virtually licensing the houses, as well as the particular occupiers. It then became inevitable that the brewers, commanding large capitals, should advance money to enable the necessary alterations to be made.[27]

Moreover, loans

> were required to pay for something which was in its nature precarious, because it depended on a licence which could at all times be lost through misconduct, and, at a later date merely because the Justices considered the house redundant. The insecurity of the licence, therefore, mitigated against obtaining capital from anyone who was not going to obtain a trading advantage from the loan, and also made the wholesalers desirous of sufficient control over the licence to prevent the possible loss of their investment.[28]

For these reasons the loan-tie was an early feature of commercial brewing and was well established throughout England by the time the 1817 Select Committee reported on conditions in the trade.[29] This Committee noted that about one half of the public houses in London were tied, and out of 48,000 licensed alehouses in the country at large, 14,200 were similarly tied through loan arrangements and brewer-ownership.

Nevertheless, up to the 1870s the rapid growth of demand for beer, reinforced by the permissive framework of licensing, enabled many brewery concerns, most notably the Burton brewers, to expand their trade without becoming too actively involved in the retail market. During the last quarter of the century, however, a rapid expansion of tied trade occurred which by 1900 had left only about 10 per cent of the total number of houses 'free'. From contemporary estimates, taking into account the substantial increase in the market value of licensed property between 1869 and 1900, the brewers' investment in public houses increased from under £30 million to well over £200 million in 30 years.[30] The brewers were no longer merely suppliers of beer, they were the owners of an extensive licensed estate.

What caused such a dramatic re-orientation of the brewers' business strategy? The traditional explanation of brewer involvement in the retail trade readily springs to mind. The re-introduction of restrictive licensing in 1869 in the form of the Beer and Wine Act was undoubtedly an important influence on the acceleration of the tied house system.[31] By curbing the growth of public houses, thereby giving licensed property a higher scarcity value, the legislature in effect compelled the brewers to buy retail outlets in order to safeguard their trade. The effects of licensing policy *per se,* however, can easily be exaggerated. An even more important catalytic factor was undoubtedly the change in market climate. As we noted in the previous section, the rapid expansion of the industry in the mid-Victorian period owed more to the great upsurge in the demand for beer than the permissive framework of licensing. Licensing policy eased the process of growth, but it was not the major causative factor. By the same token it can be argued that what primarily caused the brewers to 'safeguard their trade' from the late 1870s onwards was the deterioration in market demand which intensified competitive pressures. Between 1860 and 1880 many brewery companies greatly extended their productive capacity in order to meet the rapid growth in demand, which they had assumed would continue further. After the boom years of 1870-76, however, beer consumption slipped back and stayed on a lower plateau throughout the 1880s.

Up to 1880 a rise in real wages had tended to produce a more than proportionate increase in the consumption of beer. During the 1880s, by contrast, while real wages rose sharply, (Table 2.1), beer output virtually stagnated and *per capita* consumption actually fell. Between 1890 and 1900 the old relationship was established, but was not as strong as formerly. From 1900 onwards, real wages fell and *per capita* consumption resumed its decline, so that on the eve of the First World War it was only marginally higher than it had been in the early 1880s. The reasons for this decline in *per capita* consumption were both economic and social. A substantial fall in food prices and the availability of an increasing range of cheap mass-produced consumer goods brought about a reduction in the proportion of working-class budgets spent on beer[32]; social and recreational horizons widened, and the public house, although remaining the focal point of working-class leisure pursuits, found itself increasingly in competition from the music hall, football matches and even day railway excursions.

The concurrence of stagnating demand and the re-introduction of restrictive licensing increased competitive pressures and produced a 'domino' effect in respect of publis house acquisition. To begin with it was the provincial brewers who looked to secure their positions in this way; the Burton brewers too could no longer rely on the quantity and prestige of their beers to sell themselves as the number of 'free' outlets dried up. Finally, the main London brewers, who had hitherto stood aloof from these developments, were forced to convert their loan-ties into formal acquisitions to prevent them falling into the hands of their competitors.

The buying-up of public houses proved a costly process, as competitive bidding and the declining number of 'free' houses pushed up prices. Without the assistance of recent innovations in company financing such a large-scale expansion of the brewers' licensed estate would not have been possible. The protection of shareholders' investment by the Limited Liability Acts in the 1850s, however, had opened up new possibilities for small private family businesses to 'go public' by obtaining a Stock Exchange quotation.[33] In this respect, the brewers were in an ideal position to establish themselves as joint-stock companies; they had local, and sometimes, national reputations as prosperous businesses, and most of their capital assets were in real property.[34] Companies were floated both to facilitate the purchase of public houses by individual brewers, and also to allow a number of brewing concerns to merge their interests in order to take advantage of a chain of public houses. Thus we see here that acquisitions of public houses was one response to the problem of over-capacity, while the merger of brewing firms themselves and the closing down of redundant breweries was another.

The Growth of the Tied Trade in the Provinces

Prior to the 1880s, many country brewers, although having some establishments, depended largely on the free trade. The following examples are typical: The Lion Brewery (Chester) owned 20 public houses but trade mainly with 'hotels and private family concerns in the suburbe'; Scott and Co. (Skipton, Yorkshire) had 'a large and prosperous family trade throughout the Midlands and Northern counties', while Fremlin (Maidstone) 'cultivated no public house trade'.[35]

Some of the larger provincial brewers, however, had already plunged into the tied trade, and this dependence grew in the 1880s. Many of these concerns were to turn public, and attracted investors by stressing the advantages of having tied outlets close to their breweries. In 1874, for example, the prospectus of the Luton Brewery referred to the fact that the company owned 90 licensed houses within a radius of 7 miles of the brewery, enabling the business to be 'conducted at a comparatively small cost'.[36] Similarly, Bents Brewery of Liverpool had, by the time it went public in 1890, acquired some 120 licensed houses 'within easy distance' of their brewery.

From the mid-1880s more and more brewery firms adopted limited liability status and raised money through the Stock Market, mainly by issuing debenture stock. Between 1861 and 1866 only 20 brewery concerns became public companies. From 1886 to 1892, however, 85 firms were incorporated and in the last eight years of the century a further 149 firms followed suit.[37] Competition to buy the remaining stock of free houses consequently increased. For a brewer to ignore this process, which inevitably became cumulative, was to court disaster. The Chairman of Henry Mitchell told shareholders in his address in 1889 that, owing to the purchase of houses by other firms, the increasing competition and the falling-off in the consumption of beer generally, the company had started the year 1888-89 with a considerably decreased business but that they had recovered the lost ground by spending some £60,000 on the purchase of 70 public houses. By 1892 Mitchell owned over 200 houses.[38] Similarly, Tetley of Leeds were finding that their free trade outlets, both locally and further afield, were being absorbed by other brewers: 'In sheer self-defence the firm had to adopt the policy of other breweries else suffer severe diminution of its trade and fortunes . . .'[39]

Initially, in many cases, the competitive scramble for licensed property was directed towards consolidating the local base of the acquirer in the interests of securing economies of 'compactedness'. Later, as free houses became rarer, firms found themselves forced to look outside their immediate territories to augment their tied trade. In Burnley, for example, it was reported that by 1890 all the free houses in the town had been purchased by local brewers.[40] Two years later, Massey, who were the largest brewing concern in Burnley with some 125 houses, bought 8 public houses all of which were over 50 miles from their brewery. In short, many firms had to pay out large sums simply to defend their existing trade, while others felt it desirable to purchase property in remoter trading areas despite the heavier delivery costs involved.

Brewer ownership of licensed houses grew rapidly after 1880, but it is worthwhile noting that until the mid-1890s the growth of tied trade was much more the result of the activities of provincial brewers than of the London and Burton brewers. A report by the Home Office in 1892 revealed that in England and Wales 76 brewing companies (32 public and 44 private) owned over 100 licensed houses each,* amounting in total to 12,614 houses (12 per cent of the total number of public houses);[41] a further 165 concerns owned between 51 and 100 public houses, and 789 concerns owned between 11 and 50 public houses. Of the 76 companies who owned over 100 houses, only 10 were based in London and 2 in Burton.

The relative importance of the tie in the various regions of England and Wales is not accurately known, but some indication is given by the evidence put to the Royal Commission on Licensing (1896-99).[42] In Birmingham, for example, it was estimated that in 1896, of the city's 1,885 on-licences, around 1,500 were owned by 23 brewing companies; most of Newcastle's 598 on-licences were said to be in the hands of about a dozen firms; it was estimated that about 90 per cent of Hull's 480 on-licences were tied and the same proportion was quoted in respect of Plymouth and Bristol. Even in Leeds, where the number of free houses had long been exceptionally high for an industrial city, tied trade was increasing and by 1897 there were 285 tied houses to 478 free ones. The contrast between town and country at this time is illustrated by the figures for Cheshire. In the county as a whole it was submitted that 900 on-licences were tied and 689 were free, but in Chester itself some 80 per cent of the houses were tied. Similarly, it was submitted that of 5,418 licences of all kinds in the county of Lancashire, 3,454 were tied; in Manchester, however, about 90 per cent of the city's 3,000 licences were tied. In Yorkshire, where the overall concentration of ownership was relatively low in the early 1890s, 70 per cent of Halifax's

---

*The 12 largest owners at this time were: Greenall Whitley and Co. (681 houses), Steward and Co. (473), Peter Walker and Sons Ltd. (410), Bristol Brewery Georges Ltd. (350), Colchester Brewery Co. Ltd. (289), Truman, Hanbury Buxton Ltd. (267), Bullard and Co. (260), Watney and Co. Ltd. (258), Phipps and Co. Ltd. (242), Thwaites and Co. (219), Threlfall and Co. (213), Boddingtons Brewery Co. Ltd. (212).

603 houses were tied and 97 of Barnsley's 102 houses were tied.

Although the Commission took very little evidence from the brewers themselves on the growth of the tied trade, the figures listed in Table 2.4 indicate that the ownership of licensed property had become an increasingly significant part of most provincial brewers' operations.

Table 2.4 Value of property owned by brewery companies in 1894

Company	Capital employed 1894 (£)	Balance Sheet value of properties in 1894 (£)	Property value as % of capital
Arnold Perrett & Co. Ltd	632,000	400,402	63
Bath Brewery Co Ltd.	171,000	137,300	80
Bentley's Yorkshire Breweries Ltd.	776,000	602,000	77
Bent's Brewery Co. Ltd.	615,000	543,000	88
Bristol United Breweries Ltd.	333,000	220,000	66
Brown (Matthew) & Co. Ltd.	249,000	204,000	82
Forest Hill Brewery Co. Ltd.	77,500	53,743	70
Hancock & Co. Ltd.	455,000	186,270	41
Hardy's Crown Brewery Ltd.	655,000	416,500	63
Hodgson's Kingston Brewery Ltd.	416,000	292,000	70
Hole & Co. Ltd.	206,000	136,000	66
Kirkstall Brewery Co. Ltd.	176,000	115,750	65
Manchester Brewery Co. Ltd.	818,000	715,000	87
Nalder & Collyer Ltd.	498,000	451,000	90
Oakhill Brewery Co. Ltd.	242,000	99,600	41
Offiler's Brewery Ltd.	90,000	64,000	71
Reid, W. B. & Co. Ltd.	496,000	416,000	84
Showell's Brewery Co. Ltd.	791,000	582,500	73
Swansea United Breweries Ltd.	110,000	48,400	43
Threlfall's Brewery Co. Ltd.	1,677,000	1,281,134	76
Average			70

Source: *Brewery Manual*, 1894.

The Growth of Tied Trade in Burton and London

As the provincial brewers became increasingly committed to the ownership of retail otulets, so the other two sections of the wholesale trade, the Burton and London brewers, found their free and loan trade markets under attack. By the mid-1880s the Burton brewers especially were beginning to feel the effects of the spread fo the tied trade in their traditional markets. We have noted that the Burton brewers initially owned no houses of their own, relying instead on a national network of wholesalers and bottlers who acted as their local agents in supplying their branded pale and bitter ales to public houses. Such was the prestige of the Burton brews at this time that licensees, many of whom were loan-tied to other brewers, were more or less obliged to carry at least one of these leading brands. Increasingly, however, the provincial brewers themselves became proficient in the art of producing Burton-type ales, and, with the rapid spread of the tied house system, the major Burton brewers, especially Allsopp, found their beer excluded from other houses. This development inevitably led to fiercer competition between the Burton brewers for a diminishing number of free trade accounts. In London too, the Burton brewers were feeling the pinch as competition in loan-ties built up. The depressed state of the London market and the growth of tied trade in the provinces combined, for example, to reduce Bass's annual sales in the mid-1880s by about 100,000 barrels compared with the level achieved in the late 1870s. In such circumstances it was not long before Bass, Worthington and most of the other Burton firms entered the property market. Bass was floated as a public company in 1888 to raise funds both to extend its loan-tie business (originally started in the 1870s) and to purchase selected licensed houses in the Midlands, London, South Wales and the North East.[43] By 1900 Bass had built up a tied estate of some 550 houses. This policy, together with a more aggressive approach to obtaining representation in the tied houses of other brewers, was reflected in an improvement of the company's sales performance during the 1890s, with annual output increasing from 1,034,000 barrels in 1891 to a peak of 1,356,700 barrels in 1900.

Some of the smaller Burton brewers like Worthington and James Eadie were also able to maintain profitable trading, but others like the Burton Brewery, Nunneley and Thomas Salt, who sold most of their beer in the London market, found their sales declining.[44] Among the Burton brewers, however, it was the second largest concern, Allsopp, which suffered most and this was largely due to its initial refusal to acquire houses. When the company was floated in 1887 it owned no licensed property at all and, unlike Bass, had very little invested in loans to publicans. The directors' view that 'their beers were the best in the world' and would 'sell themselves' proved ill-founded. Between 1884 and 1891 Allsopp's output almost halved — from 824,600 barrels in 1884 to under 540,000 in 1891. From the early 1890s, therefore, the company began to acquire public houses and by 1902 it owned some 1,200 houses, which put it in second place in the property ownership 'league' behind Watney, Combe and Reid. Although sales recovered, the cost of servicing the large issue of debenture stock and shares which had been used to finance these acquisitions left Allsopp, like many other companies at this time, with very little profit.[45]

The position in London was also to change. It was noted previously that the London custom of financing the retail trade by loans was well-established in the early part of the nineteenth century. Before 1890, less than one-fifth of the public houses in London were owned by the brewers.[46] Nearly all London publicans in fact owned the leases of their houses, but because the market value of these leases was high they usually obtained a large part of the purchase price on mortgage from a brewer, who expected to receive the publican's custom for his beers. Until the 1880s loan arrangements worked well for both brewers and licensees. Without a brewer's loan the vast majority of publicans could neither have entered nor have carried on their trade. If they became dissatisfied with the beer supplied by their brewer-creditor, they could easily transfer their debt to another brewer.

In the 1880s, however, things began to alter. The decline in beer consumption was felt particularly heavily by the brewers and publicans in Central London, who were also confronted with a steady loss of customers as a result of migration to the suburbs. Some publicans became insolvent and their mortgages passed over to the brewers; many others resorted to the 'long-pull' (that is, giving customers an over-measure for the standard price) and 'diluting' their beer. At the same time, the London brewers were facing increasingly strong competition from Burton beers and were compelled in 1887 to reduce the price of their porter and mild ales. Their main competitive response, however, was to increase their investment in publicans' loans. Whitbread, for example, increased its loans from £450,000 in 1869 to £1.5 million in the early 1890s., and other leading London brewers like Truman, Reid, Meux and Combe all raised money through the Stock Market to extend their loan commitments. Down to 1895 there was no strong trend to acquire public houses; the largest owner of licensed property at this time was Truman (267 houses), followed by Watney (258), City of London Brewery (147), Taylor Walker (117) and Meux (105), but the proportion of their business going through their own houses was small in comparison with the provincial brewers.[47]

The larger London brewers still regarded themselves as brewers rather than owners of property. What made them change their thinking was the active intervention in the property market of some of the smaller London brewers in the late 1890s. These brewers were more vulnerable to falling demand and used incorporation and the offer of debentures and shares as a means of acquiring public houses, many of which had been originally loan-tied to the larger concerns. Firms who took the initiative in this way in the period 1895-98 included Charrington, Cannon Brewery, Wenlock Brewery and Noakes. Thus, as a result of the strategy adopted by the smaller brewers, the leading London brewers found themselves obliged to safeguard their trade by outright purchase of the leases of those houses on which they had already lent money. Between 1895 and 1902 the London brewers as a whole were buying up some 500 leases per year, and by 1902 some 80-85 per cent of the trade of the leading concerns was going through their own houses.[48]

The Tied Public House System and the Joint Stock Boom 1886-1900

The purchase of licensed houses, we have noted, was the only effective way in which brewery companies in the last quarter of the nineteenth century could hope to increase their sales and profits in a stagnant or at best slowly growing market. Licensed property could be bought either in the open market as private landlords chose to offer it for sale,[49] or through the acquisition of other brewery businesses with tied houses. Some companies pursued both strategies during the 1880s and 1890s; many others simply relied on buying suitable houses as they became available. Both strategies had important financial implications. As the price of licensed property rose rapidly in the 1880s, so it became increasingly difficult for many brewers to finance purchases from their own resources. In these circumstances the case for converting proprietorships and private partnerships into limited liability companies became convincing, and from 1886 both the acquisition of licensed property and mergers between brewery companies were increasingly financed by issuing debenture stock, and to a lesser extent share capital, to the public. Notwithstanding the changing trade climate, most of these issues were readily taken up by the investing public for a growing proportion of the industry's assets was in the form of licensed properties, whose value was appreciating year by year, and the national image of the brewing industry at this time was one of a secure and profitable investment.

Between 1886 and 1900 some 260 brewery concerns went public and £185 million's worth of debentures and share capital was issued. The major stock market flotations were those of the large wholesale brewers. Arthur Guinness and Ind Coope came to the market in 1886 and were followed by some of the main London brewers, and by Bass and Allsopp. Many provincial concerns, however, were also floated and a great number of these were based on the amalgamation of three, four or five businesses in order to provide a large enough basis for a public issue.[50] For instance, in 1890 four local breweries on Tyneside incorporated themselves as Newcastle Breweries Ltd.; Bristol United Brewery was established in 1889 through the amalgamation of four firms, to which others were added; Plymouth United Breweries, also formed in 1889, consisted of five local firms, while the formation of Northampton Breweries involved the amalgamation of three firms. Mergers of this kind usually allowed some breweries to be closed, with the remainder brewing for the enlarged retail network.

Management of the Tied Estate

Despite the number and spectacular nature of brewery flotations at this time, the majority of firms remained in private hands, and those that did venture to 'go public' were careful to prevent the loss of traditional family control to 'outsiders'. This they did by issuing non-voting preference shares and, more importantly, debentures. In this respect, the brewers followed the general pattern of flotations in manufacturing industry.[51]

There was thus no radical change in the management style of brewery concerns, but the tied public house system itself involved a fundamental alteration in the brewer-licensee relationship. The independent publican was replaced in the main by a 'tied tenant', and to a much lesser extent by managers.[52] In the case of tenancies, the brewer provided most of the capital, including all that which was embodied in the fabric of the building, with tenants financing their stock, fixtures and fittings. This arrangement, which remained a characteristic feature of the industry until recently can be likened to a from of 'co-partnership' in which both the brewer and his tenant had an equity interest in the business of the public house and both shared in the income that resulted from their joint activity. The brewer normally charged the tenant a low fixed rent (often referred to as the 'dry rent') and a 'surcharge' on the beer he supplied — the so-called 'wet rent' element. The tenant for his part was, of course, contracted to sell mainly his landlord's own beers, although he was permitted to sell a limited range of 'foreign' beers in cases where his landlord-brewer had entered into supply agreements with other brewers. The tenant could usually exercise his own choice from the range of his landlord's brews, but was expected to stock at least one of each main type of beer. Public bar prices were normally set by the brewer, but tenants were usually free to determine their own retail prices for other bars.

To summarise, from the late 1870s onwards the conditions which had produced the boom in the demand for beer during the mid-Victorian era began to disappear. Changing economic and social circumstances combined to produce a significant alteration in the consumption habits of the principal consumers of beer, namely, urban working men. The consumption of beer stagnated in the 1880s, partially revived in the early 1890s, and then declined. The problem for the brewers was that during the boom years the industry had greatly expanded its productive capacity on the assumption that growth would continue. The brewers response to the threat of declining output and profits was to secure their market positions by greater investment in the retail trade. Thus, it was the deterioration in the brewers' market environment that was the critical factor leading to the rapid spread of the tied public house system after 1880, rather than the change in the bias of licensing policy. The re-introduction of restrictive licensing, however, encouraged the process because it not only limited the total number of licences available (and hence made the danger of exclusion from the market more serious) but it also, significantly, placed no restrictions on the number of licences any one individual brewer could acquire. By contrast, in Scotland, where direct brewer control of the licensed outlets was to remain small, the magistrates' strong adherence to the principle of 'one man, one licence' effectively limited the scope for public house acquisition.

Thus, in England and Wales the end of market growth brought with it a significant change in the nature of competition within the brewing industry. While the promotion of product quality and prestige remained important, competition increasingly revolved around the acquisition of public houses. In a limited sense, of course, the expansion of the tied public house system can be viewed as being ultimately 'anti-competitive', that is, as a result of the formal acquisition of a house by a particular brewer, other brewers' beers are excluded from it. Viewed in the context of the circumstances of the brewing industry in the last quarter of the nineteenth century, however, the process must be looked upon somewhat differently. Given the fact that his competitors were buying up outlets, no brewer (unless, like Guinness, his beer was in a category of its own) could afford not to do likewise if he were to survive. In this more general sense, *forward integration far from suppressing competition was essential to its continuance.* Moreover, the fact that the retail trade in urban areas was increasingly dominated by local brewers whose market presence was based on property ownership, did not destroy the concept of a national market above and beyond the tied house system. The largest brewery company in the country, Arthur Guinness, as we have noted, maintained a solid rate of growth throughout the period despite owning no licensed property. The key to Guinness's success was product differentiation. The company's stout, sold mainly in bottled form, attracted a strong and loyal clientele, and since no English brewer sought to compete directly with Guinness for this sector of the market, Guinness, like the lager firms in the late 1950s and 1960s, was able to take full advantage of the wide distribution accorded by the tied house system.

The Industry in the Depressed Years: 1900—14
The Economic and Financial Problems of the Industry
Even before the end of the nineteenth century it had become obvious that the industry was heading for more difficult times. The cost of acquiring public houses had risen steeply and the demand for beer, although it had recovered somewhat from the 1880s, was not great enough to sustain all of the substantial number of public houses in industrial areas, many of which were concentrated in old, declining, 'inner city' areas. Excess competition in the retail trade was rife and brewers' profit margins had shrunk.

From 1900 onwards, the economic depression served to exacerbate the financial problems of the brewing industry as well as other important industries. Real wages stopped rising and the demand for beer fell. Between 1900 and 1913 the population of the UK grew by nearly 13 per cent but total beer consumption fell by over 5 per cent. In *per capita* terms, therefore, the decline was much more pronounced, falling from 31.7 gallons in 1893-1900 to 27.3 gallons in 1911-13 (see Table 2.1).

The combination of a fall in demand for beer and excess productive capacity inevitably led to lower profits. Furthermore, the financial pressure on brewery companies at this time was compounded by the legacy of costly public house acquisitions. The brewers had paid for them, it was noted above, by issuing considerable amounts of debenture stock and preference shares. As sales fell the brewers found increasing difficulty in meeting interest and dividend payments and were forced in many cases to alter their capital structures.[53]

While it was principally the fall in demand which hindered the brewers' attempt to improve the return on their licensed estate, the situation was not helped by the management difficulties of running an integrated business. Apart from ensuring that the 'tie' was properly observed, considerable problems were encountered in finding suitable tenants to run their houses.[54] Several additional sources of financial strain in regard to the licensed estate may be noted. The 1904 Licensing

Act had established a 'compensation fund' to pay off publicans whose licences were not renewed and this was financed by a levy on every licensed house; more importantly, the brewers were having to spend money on improving the general state of their public houses, most of which had, prior to their acquisition, become run-down and dilapidated;[55] and in 1909, the Government imposed a drastic increase in the rate of duty payable on retail licences.[56] As noted above, a fundamental change in licensing policy was also to affect the position of the brewers during this period, and beyond. As a result of some laxness in the administration of the 1869 Act, the reduction in the number of licensed premises down to the late 1890s had not been substantial. Following on, however, from the re-affirmation of the right of magistrates to close public houses on the grounds that they were surplus to the requirements of the locality (*Sharpe* v *Wakefield*, 1891) and the growing influence of the temperance lobby within the Liberal party, a tougher line was taken with regard to renewal applications.[57] This was to culminate in 1904 with the passing of a new licensing Act which established a statutory principle of public house closure in areas where, on social grounds, they were considered to be superfluous.[58] The Act did not, however, envisage a wholesale suppression of the beer trade as advocated by the temperance movement. Rather, the philosophy embodied in the Act was essentially gradualist and pragmatic and its application was to be consistent with the 'legitimate' right of the industry to ply its trade whilst nevertheless being beneficial for the social order.[59]

The effect of the Act was thus to accelerate the trend of public house closures; the licensing returns indicate that between 1906 (when the Act was fully implemented) and 1914, 3,736 fully-licensed houses and 5,881 beerhouses were shut down, amounting to an overall reduction of nearly 10 per cent in the number of on-licenses.[60] Most of the reductions occurred before 1910. Looked at from a longer term perspective, it can be argued that the reduction in the number of public houses was not at odds with the industry's basic need, namely, the elimination of uneconomic retail outlets because of a lower level of demand. There is no doubt that even without licensing intervention, the brewers themselves would have been forced to close down a portion of their tied estate.[61]

The short-term problem, however, was how to secure a reduction in the number of public houses without causing severe financial losses to the brewers who had invested so much capital in them. (Because of depressed property values this was only partially resolved by compensation arrangements.) Another important consideration was the problem

facing some brewers, particularly those whose trade was centred on declining 'inner city' areas, in adjusting to shifting population patterns.
Given the justices' remit to reduce the overall number of licensed houses,
together with the fragmented and local nature of licensing applications,
there was insufficient flexibility to ensure that licence reduction in
areas of superfluity was matched by new licences in expanding districts.
A further complication was introduced into the industry's affairs by the
fact that the 1904 Act discriminated against public houses to the advantage of licensed clubs, then posing a growing competitive threat
to the established retail trade.[62]

Competition and Concentration

The stagnation of the beer market in the last quarter of the nineteenth
century, it will be recalled, had intensified competitive pressures. The
brewers had responded to the prospects of declining sales and profits
by purchasing licensed premises. Brewers competed strenuously with
one another to secure viable market access. By 1900, with all but 10
per cent of public houses in the hands of the brewers, this type of competitive initiative was all but over. Thus, the brewers were unable to
adapt to the even greater deterioration in their market during the first
decade and a half of the new century in the same way as they had in
the previous period. By this time anyway, there were too many licensed
houses in relation to demand so it is a moot point whether the process
of acquisition would have been extended further even if restrictive
licensing had not curtailed the establishment of new outlets.

Instead, brewers and publicans were forced to channel their competitive efforts in other ways. The 'long pull' (giving more beer for the
same 'standard' price) became even more widespread than it had been
formerly; although the brewers disliked the practice they came to
regard it as a fact of life, and were forced in turn to subsidise their
tenants by charging low rentals.[63] Direct retail price competition also
came to a head, but was never as aggressive as it might have been in the
circumstances. Some concerted price restraint was exercised, but in the
main the desire to avoid price competition reflected the already poor
state of trade and the insensitivity of demand to price cuts. Nor would
price-cutting have been to the liking of the temperance lobby. A more
effective long-term way of securing custom than the provision of 'cheap
beer' was seen to be investment in improving the standards of public
houses and, as we have noted, many brewers had already made a start
in this direction. Had 'teetotal' magistrates also subscribed to the view
that improved public houses was the 'social' answer to drink abuse,

then brewer competition at this time would without doubt have centred upon this aspect, as indeed happened after 1918. In the event, however, many magistrates strongly resisted the attempt to improve public houses. Applications from brewers and licensees to improve the level of amenities provided in individual public houses, which involved re-arranging the internal structure of the premises, or creating additional space, were usually rejected on the grounds that they also provided 'increased facilities for drinking'. Moreover, the brewer often found that if an application for improvement was not rejected out of hand, it would be made conditional on the voluntary surrender of one or more licensed houses which had not hitherto been closed through the compensation procedure. Consequently, many brewers were discouraged by the cost of the *quid pro quo* from attempting to refurbish houses.[64]

Not only were the brewers' public houses competing against each other, but increasingly, they faced a new competitive threat in the form of the growing club trade. At this time working men's clubs held several competitive advantages over the public house. They were unlicensed and hence outside magisterial control, their opening hours were unregulated, and they were less restricted in offering games facilities and other entertainments. Finally, because they paid no retail excise licence duty and were often non-profit making organisations, they were in general able to sell their beer at lower prices than the ordinary publican. With all these advantages behind them, it is hardly surprising that the number of clubs increased rapidly. From their humble origins in the 1880s the club population had risen to over 8,700 by 1914.[65] As such they provided powerful competition to public houses in urban strongholds. At the same time, however, this enlargement of the 'free trade' sector provided new growth opportunities for the brewer eager for expansion. The Burton brewers, Bass and Worthington, together with Arthur Guinness and the Scottish brewers, Wm. Youngers, were especially well placed to service the new trade, not only because of their traditional cultivation of the free trade, but also because bottled ales constituted an important element in the club trade.

Against this background of more intense competitive pressures, the period 1900-1914 saw a continuation of the trend towards greater concentration in the industry. The publican-brewer, whose numbers had already been drastically reduced, was virtually to disappear, and the larger commercial brewers began to grow at the expense of their smaller competitors. The number of brewing concerns fell from a total of 6,390 in 1900 to 3,650 in 1914. However, the process of concentration was not as rapid in this period as it had been towards the end of

the nineteenth century. Between 1888 and 1900 the number of brewing companies absorbed by other firms totalled some 215, but between
1901 and 1914 only 67 firms were absorbed. One might have expected
the rate of concentration to have increased after 1900, as the demand
for beer fell and the problem of surplus capacity became more widespread. The fact that it did not do so calls for further explanation. The
first point to note is that the reduced level of merger activity was not
peculiar to the brewing industry. The decade 1890-1900 had witnessed
a sharp rise in merger activity in many other important manufacturing
industries (chemicals, textiles and cement, for instance) which was not
maintained between 1900 and 1914. The main cause of these mergers
was heightened competitive pressures resulting from imports and the
emergence of new domestic producers, and their prime objective was to
stabilise prices at higher levels, not cut costs.[66] Few of these mergers,
however, came up to expectations and this disillusionment led to a
falling-off in merger rates after 1900. In the brewing industry, by contrast, the 'monopolisation' motive was not a significant factor in most
mergers. There was no equivalent in brewing of the giant, multi-firm
combines which were spawned in chemicals and textiles, for example,
although it is certainly true that during the course of the joint-stock
boom, as we have noted, there were some mergers involving several
local firms, which between them had a significant proportion of the
trade in their particular areas. The creation of local monopolies, however, was a rare occurrence and large scale multi-firm mergers were the
exception rather than the rule in the brewing industry. Between 1886
and 1900, 62 companies were formed and floated on the London Stock
Exchange as a result of mergers involving 175 firms — a ratio of only
1 : 2.8.

There can be little doubt, therefore, that the overriding objective of
most brewery mergers, both before and after 1900, was expansion.
Breweries were usually bought up for the licensed property they owned.
In the period before 1900 brewers interested in expansion acquired or
merged with other concerns in order to increase their sales through an
enlarged public house network. Frequently, a by-product of this process
was the closure of redundant brewery capacity, but brewery rationalisation was not normally the prime motive. After 1900, the demand for
beer declined and many companies found themselves with surplus
capacity. As noted above, the reaction of producers in certain other
industries to growing competition was to indulge in price-fixing. In
brewing, however, this was not a practical proposition. Since the 1880s,
beer had become expensive relative to other goods consumed by the

working classes, and retailers had long been under pressure to reduce their margins by resorting to the 'long pull' (which was, of course, an indirect form of price cutting). Unlike other industries, the fundamental problem facing the brewing industry was not one of imports nor the entry of new producers, but a fall in demand brought about by the changing pattern of social habits. Cost reduction was the only practical way of increasing margins and rationalisation of brewing capacity and distribution by merger and amalgamation was necessary to secure this. As the *Brewers' Gazette* observed:

> It is clear that brewing costs can be reduced by this method and the closing down of breweries within the metropolitan area and the concentration of brewing operations for a number of companies in a few of the largest and best-equipped plants would be calculated to assist in the financial regeneration of companies. . . . For with amalgamation they will in a majority of cases be associated with the extinction of capital unrepresented by assets.[67]

Concentration, however, proceeded more slowly after 1900 than it had done in the 1890s and it was largely the capital reorganisation aspects of mergers which were to prove the inhibiting factor. Ironically, the main opposition came from those debenture interests which had played such an important role in financing mergers and public house acquisitions in the late nineteenth century. It was these interests which for example prevented a tripartite merger between Allsopp, Thomas Salt and the Burton Brewery Company from going ahead in 1906, and similarly frustrated the proposed merger between Ind Coope and Allsopp in 1911. Debenture holders took a less sanguine view of the merits of mergers than did shareholders, partly because they held prior claims on the profits and assets of their existing firms, but more importantly because many mergers involved a proposed capital reconstruction in the interests of securing a 'better balance' between expected profits and assets, and this entailed diluting the debenture stock.

This is not to say, of course, that mergers had no impact at this time. Outside London and Burton some of the larger companies extended their trading positions and rationalised brewing capacity. Examples include Walker and Homfray of Salford, Bristol Brewery Georges, and Bengley's Yorkshire Breweries. Moreover, efficiency gains continued to acrue without merger through the introduction of stricter business principles, economies in the use of materials and the further application of scientific and technological aids to the production process.[68]

Nevertheless, what was required was a more radical reorganisation of the industry. When it was realised, as it came to be in the period after

1918, that the decline in demand, far from being temporary, was to prove a persistent feature, restructuring could no longer be delayed.

The Industry in the Inter-War Period
The Decline in Demand

The main impact of the First World War on the market for beer was to reinforce the trend of declining consumption and output. During the war, the permitted hours of opening for licensed premises were drastically curtailed, the duty on beer was increased sharply, so pushing up retail prices, and the brewers were requested to reduce both the volume and gravities of their beers. As a result of these measures beer output fell from 37 million bulk barrels in 1914 to 19 million bulk barrels in 1918.

After a short post-war boom in demand, the consumption of beer continued to decline and reached levels which before 1914 would have been regarded as impossibly low. In the period 1920-25, average *per capita* consumption was 35 per cent below the level of 1910-14; in 1925-30 it was 39 per cent below, and in 1931-35 it was 52 per cent below (Table 2.5). In bulk terms, of course, the fall in consumption was less dramatic. Nevertheless by the late 1920s it was clear that a profound change had occurred in the nation's drinking habits. Some of the factors which contributed to this change have already been indicated, notably higher taxation and prices, reduced drinking hours and the diminished strength of beers. A quadrupling of the exise duty after 1918 which raised beer prices to 7 pence a pint by 1922 (double the pre-war level), obviously contributed significantly to reducing total beer consumption. It also affected the pattern of consumption to some extent

Table 2.5 *Beer output and consumption, 1900-39*

	Beer output in millions (standard barrels)	Consumption per head (gallons)
1900-4	35.2	30.2
1905-9	33.2	27.3
1910-14	34.1	26.9
1915-19	22.7	16.5
1920-24	22.3	16.4
1925-29	20.3	16.3
1930-34	16.6	13.0
1935-39	16.9	13.2

Source: B. R. Mitchell and P. Deane, *Abstracts of British Historical Statistics*, Cambridge University Press, 1962.

by producing a shift in demand to the cheaper mild ales. However, it was also the case at this time that the public was demanding increasing quantities of relatively more expensive bottled beer. Thus, a purely economic interpretation of the change in consumption habits is inadequate. In particular, the failure of beer consumption to respond to rising real incomes in the late 1920s suggests that fundamental changes had also occurred in popular attitudes, not only towards drink itself but also towards the role of the public house as a social institution.

The trend towards 'moderation and sobriety' at this time was clearly reflected in a sustained, nationwide decline in the level of drunkenness; convictions for drunkenness fell from an average of 195,000 in 1910-14 to an average of under 45,000 in 1930-35.[69] It was also reflected in the fact that there was no strong public demand for the relaxation of the restrictions on opening hours which were continued after the war, nor a backlash to 'weaker' beers. As the Royal Commission (1929-31) observed:

> We have found a remarkable consensus in favour of restriction. . . .
> We think that to a vast section of the public, including public house clients, the present scheme is acceptable and is becoming more, not less so. That such is the case is, in our opinion, vital. Restriction in a matter of this kind depends on the sanction of public opinion'.[70]

Moreover, the position of the public house as the social centre of the working classes was being increasingly challenged by the growth of alternative forms of leisure activities such as the cinema, radio and sport.

Improvements too in the urban environment served to 'break the association between bad housing and heavy drinking which had been a feature of the Victorian era, and resulted in a shift in the pattern of working class spending increasingly towards items for the house.[71] Between 1911 and 1939 some 5 million new houses were built. Much of this building occurred on the suburban fringes of the major conurbations and gave a strong push to the centrifugal movement of population which had begun within these conurbations towards the end of the nineteenth century. Suburban society contained several features which stood in marked contrast to the pattern of life in the Victorian working class areas. Family sizes were smaller, physical conditions healthier, and social aspirations markedly broader.

Licensing and State Regulation

In addition to the poor state of trade, another factor which had an important bearing on the brewers' business conduct at this time was their growing sensitivity to the temperance lobby. The new concern may seem surprising in view of the fact that the application of restrictive licensing down the years had specifically recognised the right of the brewers to ply their trade within a framework of social control, and that they had for so long warded off attempts by the temperance movement to have the trade suppressed.

The new consideration that heightened the long-standing controversy over the compatability of the brewers' pursuit of profits and the social order was the 'nationalisation' of the trade in and around the Carlisle area during the war. The 'Carlisle scheme', which was originally introduced in an attempt to control excessive drinking by construction workers building a vital munitions factory, was continued after the war.[72] In conception, the scheme was primarily a social experiment, its objective being to rationalise and improve the licensed trade in the interests of temperance. Significantly, the 'new style' management adopted the policy of the brewers themselves when they embraced the philosophy of 'fewer and better' public houses as a means of promoting civilised drinking; superfluous houses were closed down and the remaining ones improved. The scheme, however, had economic overtones. Not only did it make a modest profit, but it facilitated the process of brewery rationalisation; the Control Board had acquired five breweries in the district but quickly closed down three of them.

The combination of these social and economic benefits arising from the scheme thus provided a powerful platform for the claims of those who believed that an extension of State management would improve the condition of the industry much faster and more effectively than the brewers themselves were able to do.[73] Whatever the merits of this argument, however, the idea of total public ownership and State monopoly was alien to the political economy philosophies of the day and the matter was not pursued further.

In addition, there was at this time a strong undercurrent of popular belief that the brewers had abused their control of the trade by 'profiteering' at the expense of the public, by driving out independent licensees and by subjecting those that remained to onerous conditions.[74] This belief was partially embraced by the Royal Commission (1929-31) who, like future official investigators of the industry, considered (in our view, erroneously) that the tied public house system operated only to the advantage of the brewers and had very little positive to offer to the licensee or the consuming public.[75] They did, however, accept that the 'tie' was a fundamental feature of the industry, and thereby dismissed the idea of prohibiting it.

All in all then these were difficult times for the industry and the challenge posed for the brewers was one of adaptability. On the one hand, brewers and licensees alike had to find some way of preventing their trade from becoming locked into a situation of long-term decline. On the other hand, the prevailing climate of opinion strongly implied that the brewers should temper their commercial instincts with a sense of social responsibility. It was this attempt to reconcile conventional business objectives with the less familar norms of social responsibility which was to exercise a profound influence on the subsequent development of the industry.

Social Responsibility and the Profit Motive

The post-war changes in popular attitudes towards drinking and the public house had important implications, we have suggested, for the brewers. In terms of production, the continuing fall in demand aggravated the problem of over-capacity which in turn resulted in widespread mergers and rationalisation. This point will be discussed in the next section. In the retail trade, however, the problem posed by declining demand was more complex, being bound up also with the social issue. The number of public houses continued to decline in line with the change in licensing policy instituted by the 1904 Licensing Act and the closure of redundant houses by the brewers. In 1905 there were 98,894 public houses, but by 1935 their number had fallen to 75,528. While this reduction in the number of traditional outlets went some way to ameliorate the problem of securing adequate sales per house, competitive pressures remained intense as the clubs began to take an increasing proportion of the trade that remained, especially in the urban areas of the North, Midlands and South Wales. Over the period 1905-35 the number of clubs in England and Wales increased from 6,554 to 15,657, bringing the total membership figure to more than 5 million. As the Royal Commission observed: 'The club, in many instances has become a formidable competitor to licensed premises. In our view, a club . . . fulfils substantially the same purpose as a public house. The evidence shows that the competition of such clubs is felt keenly and greatly resented by the licensed victualler'.[76] This enlargement of the free trade sector, as noted earlier, had also presented a growth opportunity for the brewers in respect of their wholesale business and provoked intensive competition for the new trade. The standard method of establishing a club was for the promoters to solicit a loan from a brewer and promise to sell his beer in return. To this extent loan competition between brewers for club representation was similar in kind to the 'loan-tie' arrangements they had developed with publicans in the nineteenth century. However, it is to be noted that the clubs themselves had by this time entered into 'co-operative' brewing.[77]

The brewers' answer to the mounting competitive pressures and social criticisms, revolved around rehabilitating the tarnished image of the public house. Many brewers had already attempted to improve their licensed estates but, as we have noted, the process had been limited by a number of factors. After 1918, however, the concept of public house improvement attracted widespread support both within the industry as well as from social reformers. As the *Brewing Trade Review* pointed out:

> In the minds of the more thoughtful section of the industry there is no fundamental conflict between the financial interests of the licensed trade and the social environment of the people, and this social improvement can be carried out without antagonising the consumer. What we may call the backbone of this policy is the improved public house.[78]

A rough indication of the progress which the brewers had made in this direction during the 1920s may be gleaned from evidence submitted to the Royal Commission; a survey of 329 brewing companies owning a total of 47,224 public houses showed that £12.3 million was spent on building, rebuilding or otherwise improving 13,452 of them over the period 1922-26; another survey revealed that between 1927-30, 84 companies owning some 27,000 houses spent £8.6 million on similar work carried out on nearly 6,600 of them.[79] In other words, between 1922 and 1930 approximately 27 per cent of the total number of public houses in England and Wales were improved in one way or another.

The pace of improvement could, of course, have been faster, but again there were limits set not only by financial constraints but also by the continuing hostility of many magistrates to increased facilities for drinking. While, under State ownership more might have been done (although this is questionable), similar objections regarding the alleged 'subsidisation' of drinking would still have been voiced.

On the whole, brewing companies found that in the short-run the increased expense of improving their public houses was not matched by a corresponding increase in net revenue. However, as they quickly realised, a long-term view of these investments was essential. What they needed to justify this long term perspective was, of course, an assurance that this investment would be reasonably secure. Secure, that is, not from normal competitive pressures but from undue State intervention. By the 1930s with nationalisation out of favour and the solution of the divestiture of the tied estate firmly rejected, this need had largely been met.

Mergers and Rationalisation

The poor state of trade for much of the inter-war period led to a substantial reduction in the number of breweries. In 1920 the number of breweries totalled 2,889, compared to 4,482 in 1910. In 1930, their numbers had been reduced to 1,418, and by the outbreak of the Second World War the total was only 885. Mergers and acquisitions were to play an important part in this process of concentration, following the evaporation of stockholder opposition, noted earlier. Between 1915 and 1935, 283 quoted brewery companies acquired a total of 261 firms, 227 of which were absorbed between 1919 and 1932. Some companies were particularly active acquirers, notably Ind Coope (7 firms), Allsopp (6), Simonds (8), Brickwood (6), Matthew Brown (7) and Watney Combe Reid (5).

The two sections of the industry which had suffered most from over-capacity in the period 1900-14, London and Burton, were especially subject to widespread merger activity and rationalisation. In London, the few remaining middle-sized and small companies largely disappeared, and the bigger London brewers broke out of the city itself by acquiring a substantial number of smaller firms in the rapidly-expanding Home Counties area. The Burton trade experienced an equally rapid concentration centering around Bass, which acquired Worthington, Thomas Salt and James Eadie, and Ind Coope and Allsopp who merged in 1934 to form the largest brewing concern in the country. In the provinces too there was a general tendency towards greater local and in some cases regional concentration. Firms such as H. and G. Simonds (Reading), Greene King (Bury St. Edmonds), Vaux (Sunderland), Brickwood (Portsmouth) and Fremlin (Maidstone) not only bought small firms adjacent to their territories, but ventured somewhat further afield, thereby establishing quasi-regional trading areas.

A general theme running through most mergers was the need to increase or maintain output in an era of declining demand in order to enable the larger breweries to operate at viable levels of production, and this could only be achieved, given the established vertically integrated nature of the industry, by enlarging the market area serviced by the brewery through the acquisitions of the licensed houses of other brewers. As the chairman of Ind Coope noted at the time of his company's merger with Allsopp:

> In order to maintain economic and profitable business it is necessary to maintain the output of our breweries. This has only been possible by the increase in the number of licensed houses which form our distributing agencies. To achieve this, both Allsopp and

ourselves, in common with other large concerns, have acquired from time to time smaller brewing businesses whose houses have been added to our own. But the supply of small businesses is dwindling.[81]

Throughout the period in fact there was a general increase in the size of businesses which were acquired. This was due not only to the disappearance of smaller firms, but it was also due to the fact that with the development of motor transport, distribution costs were not as significant in limiting the area of the merger of the larger companies as they had been at earlier times. Both the expansion of the London brewers into the Home Counties and the emergence of regional concerns in the provinces was largely due to this factor.[82]

Changes in the pattern of the demand also helped the larger brewers to extend their influence in the trade. Bottled beer steadily increased in popularity and by the 1930s accounted for some 25 per cent of the industry's sales. The problem for the smaller brewer was not only that the bottling process itself required expensive capital outlays, but that bottled beer was costly to promote. Moreover, the larger brewers such as Ind Coope-Allsopp, Bass, Worthington and Whitbread had already established a 'national' presence in this section of the trade and a substantial number of smaller concerns were obliged to sell these 'foreign' beers in their houses because of the force of public demand.

What were the effects of mergers on the level of concentration and efficiency at this time? Regarding the former, the answer clearly is that the merger wave did not produce a significant increase in the overall level of capital concentration. Companies having a capitalisation of less than £1 million accounted for 87 per cent of the 365 public companies in 1927, falling to 74 per cent in 1942 (298 companies). (See Table 2.6.) Medium sized companies with a capitalisation in the range of £1-2.5 million increased their share over

Table 2.6 *Distribution of listed brewery companies by capital*

Size (£)	1927		1936		1942	
	No.	(%)	No.	(%)	No.	(%)
Under 1m	318	87.1	240	77.4	221	74.1
1−2.5m	32	8.7	49	15.8	56	18.8
2.5−5.0m	11	3.0	13	4.2	13	4.3
5.0−10m	3	0.8	6	1.9	6	2.0
Over 10m	1	0.4	2	0.6	2	0.8
Total	365	100	310	100	298	100

Source: Stock Exchange Year Books.

the same period from 8.7 per cent to 18.8 per cent, while larger companies with a capitalisation of over £2.5 million increased their share from 4.2 per cent to 7.1 per cent. When, in addition, account is taken of the substantial number of smaller private concerns, it is seen that the industry was still, organisationally speaking, highly fragmented. The degree of concentration, however, both nationally and regionally, was somewhat greater in output terms, corresponding to the prominence of national distributors in the bottled beer sector and regional concerns in the draught sector, but nonetheless insufficient to substantiate any strong claim of 'monopolisation'. In the mid-1930s the three largest firms accounted for only 18 per cent of the industry's net output, a figure which was much lower than in many other old-established industries.[83]

As regards efficiency, the position is more complex. Over the period 1915-39 the number of breweries fell from 3,556 to 885, mainly as a result of closures following mergers and amalgamations, while the average output of breweries rose from 9,777 barrels in 1915 to 27,881 barrels in 1939. Census of Production data suggests that the larger companies made considerable gains in efficiency and, although some of this improvement was due to organic factors, it may be inferred that much of it was due to post-merger rationalisation. Output per head, for example, for companies employing 500-749 people increased from £728 to £897 over the period 1930-35; for companies employing 750-999 the increase over the same period was from £751 to £1,067 and for companies employing over 1,000, output per head rose from £752 to £905.[84] On the other hand, the continued presence of a large 'fringe' of smaller firms could be taken as evidence that not all potential efficiency gains were fully realised. These firms, in the main family-controlled concerns, were less vulnerable to take-over and able to survive because of the protection accorded them by their tied houses. To infer, however, that all small firms are inefficient would be wrong.[85] Moreover, to judge an industry by reference to an instantaneous idealised state of efficiency without due regard to the forces which have shaped the industry's development and the time required to 'digest' and implement change, is equally amiss. As a study of British industry by Hannah has emphasised, the tendency towards 'conservatism' with regard to restructuring and rationalisation was by no means peculiar to the brewing industry during the inter-war period.[86]

In conclusion, therefore, it could be argued that during the first half of the twentieth century the brewers made a virtue of necessity. The trend of demand was downwards and the public house was losing its appeal as a social centre; restrictive licensing had become tighter and state ownership of the industry was being canvassed. In short, the industry was on the defensive and had to prove that its continued existence was compatible with the public interest. It did so by embracing the concept of social responsibility and by fostering structural change. While the requirements of socially responsible management could be used to justify investment decisions which would only be profitable in the long term, the brewers saw no inherent conflict between these requirements and the profit motive. The congruence of commercial and social criteria may therefore be seen as an example of Adam Smith's 'invisible hand', which harnesses private interest to the public good. This is certainly how the brewers themselves tended to view their own positions and, given the legal and social constraints within which the industry was compelled to operate, it is difficult to see how they could have adopted any other perspective.

3 Developments in the Industry Since 1950

In the 30 years following the end of the Second World War the market trends outlined in the preceding chapter became even more pronounced. The period as a whole witnessed an unprecedented increase in living standards, yet it was not until after about 1959 that the brewing industry began to benefit from this improvement. After a brief recovery during the war years beer consumption resumed its downward trend until the late 1950s when this trend was halted and then reversed. In the decade 1965-75 beer consumption grew on average by 3 per cent a year. What, then, lay behind this sudden and, in historical terms, extremely significant change in the industry's market? Firstly, it would seem that the brewers' response to the challenge posed by the market revolution of the inter-war years became increasingly effective during the post-war period, especially after 1960. The brewers extended their commercial interests beyond the production of beer and the ownership of public houses. The industry as a whole was increasingly seen to be part of a much wider and highly competitive leisure market. The growing force of external competition in turn had far-reaching effects on competitive behaviour within the industry. The dominance of tied trade became less marked and the importance of the free market correspondingly increased. The normative force of tradition declined, particularly in the field of property management. The brewers' need to compete more effectively within the leisure market called for additional resources, which in turn generated further changes in the structure and conduct of the industry. Yet the brewers' efforts to improve their competitive position did not win universal approval. Many observers feared that the concentration of both the production of beer and the ownership of public houses in fewer and fewer hands was not in the public interest. Paradoxically, therefore, the growth of competitive behaviour within the brewing industry during this period provoked a sustained debate over whether or not the State should intervene in order to promote more competition.

The Growth of a National Market

Ever since the development of a nation-wide railway network in the middle decades of the nineteenth century there has been a national market for beer. The growth of the tied-house system, however, restricted that market to the handful of brewery companies (Guinness, Bass, Worthington, Ind Coope, Allsopp and Whitbread) whose beers had already achieved something approaching national status. From 1900 onwards this small and competitive national market was dominated by a few well-known brands of bottled stout and pale ale. Local brewers took these brands from the national or quasi-national companies and sold them through their own tied houses. The swing towards bottled beer during the inter-war period increased the significance of the national market and encouraged those companies who supplied it to expand and intensify their geographical coverage through amalgamations and reciprocal trading agreements. This trend continued during the post-war decade. During the 1930s bottled beer had accounted for about 25 per cent of total consumption by value; further growth took this proportion to just over 50 per cent by the mid-1950s.[1] The national brewers supplied about half the sales of bottled beer in the immediate post-war period, or, in other words, one quarter of total beer sales by value.[2] This market position had been built up partly by further amalgamations. Thus by 1950, Ind Coope and Allsopp controlled 19 subsidiary companies, Bass controlled 13 and Watney controlled 7. Reciprocal trading agreements, however, were also important. Whitbread were the leading practicioners of this strategy, which they preferred to the more conventional method of expanding through direct acquisition. The company frequently cemented these arrangements by acquiring a small but significant share of a trading partner's equity. Bass had initiated this policy during the inter-war period but it was Whitbread who really applied it on a national scale. Between 1945 and 1960 they acquired 'umbrella' holdings (usually in the order of 15-25 per cent of the equity) in no fewer than twenty quoted brewery companies situated throughout the UK. This policy gave them all the advantages of national distribution without the costs of acquiring and managing a national chain of public houses. As Col. W. H. Whitbread informed his shareholders in 1955:

> Throughout the industry the demand for high quality bottled beers continues to grow at the expense of draught beers . . . your company's bottled beers are now stocked and sold in well over half the licensed houses in the country as a result of the consistently growing popular demand for them.

What factors account for the increasing popularity of bottled beer during the 1950s? Firstly, bottled beer continued to enjoy a decisive advantage over draught beer in terms of the consistency of its flavour and appearance. This attribute had in fact been reinforced during the Second World War, when the general shortage of raw materials had forced the brewers to use substitutes and this in turn had frequently resulted in the production of inferior and unpredictable draught beer. Bottled beer, at least in its chilled and pasteurised form, had retained its quality rather better. Secondly, bottled beer also benefitted from the growing importance of packaging. As one observer pointed out:

> All men and women aged 30 and under have been brought up in a home atmosphere where glass as a container for food and drink has been increasingly used. Gradually the public have become 'container-conscious' and they consequently have a certain bias towards drinks purveyed in a form which is at once more hygienic than in the old days and very much more dependable in quality and condition. It is not surprising, therefore, that many younger people today should have an instinctive attraction towards bottled brands of beer. They do not always appreciate the 'goodness' of what they imbibe. To them a bottle of something conveys an impression of unadulterated cleanliness and virtue.[3]

Thirdly, the rapid growth of television ownership during the 1950s greatly strengthened the trend towards home drinking. In 1947 only 0.2 per cent of the adult population possessed a television set; by 1960 nearly 82 per cent did so.[4] Home drinking naturally increased the demand for bottled beer. By the same token the continued growth of suburban housing estates, where off-licences were in general more numerous and easier to obtain than full on-licences, also stimulated bottled beer consumption.

The market strength of bottled beer in general during the 1950s and, more especially, the popularity of a relatively small number of heavily-advertised, national brands suggests that more and more beer drinkers were prepared to depart from the traditional pattern of local and regional tastes. This trend was reinforced by the development, from the late 1950s onwards, of keg beer — which in effect reproduced all the characteristics of bottled beer in draught form. Keg beer was pasteurised and was thus protected for very much longer than traditional draught beer from deterioration.[5] This protection was increased by the use of carbon dioxide in both the production stage itself and the serving of the beer across the bar. Flowers' Breweries Ltd. were the first company to produce keg beer on a significant scale, closely followed by Watney Mann, Ind Coope, Whitbread and the other national and regional brewers. The first major symptom of this change was that the demand for bottled beer after decades of steady growth, began to decline (Table 3.1).

Table 3.1 *Trends in UK beer consumption, 1959-70*
(% of total market by volume)

	1959	1964	1966	1968	1970
Draught Mild	42	33	30	28	22
Draught Bitter	21	25	26	27	28
Keg Beers	1	6	8	10	17
Lager	2	2	3	4	5
Pale/Light Ales	12	14	14	13	12
Brown Ales	12	10	9	8	6
Stout	10	10	10	10	10

Source: *E. I. U. Retail Business* Nos. 119 and 174.

In 1959 'packaged' beer (which was almost entirely in bottled form) held 36 per cent of the volume market; by 1970 this share had declined to about 27 per cent and even within the 'packaged' sector, bottled beer was steadily losing ground in favour of canned beer. The rapid growth of keg beer also had a major effect on the rest of the draught beer market

Table 3.2 *Trends in UK beer consumption, 1971-76*
(% of total market by volume)

	1971	1972	1973	1974	1975	1976
Draught						
Keg Bitter and Stout	17.4	17.8	17.0	16.8	15.9	15.2
Ordinary Bitter	31.3	31.1	30.5	30.5	30.9	30.7
Mild	17.7	15.9	14.2	13.8	13.3	12.5
Lager	7.1	8.6	11.3	12.7	15.6	18.6
Total draught	73.5	73.4	73.0	73.8	75.7	77.0
Packaged						
Lager	2.8	3.1	3.6	3.7	4.3	5.2
Light/Pale Ale	11.5	11.4	11.9	11.7	10.9	9.9
Brown	4.0	3.9	3.7	3.5	2.8	2.4
Stout	7.0	6.8	6.4	5.9	5.0	4.2
Others	1.2	1.4	1.4	1.4	1.3	1.3
Total packaged	26.5	26.6	27.0	26.2	24.2	23.0

Source: The Brewers' Society: Price Commission Report No. 31, p. 2.

as more and more traditional draught beers were subject to 'pressurication' (but not pasteurisation) through the introduction of carbon dioxide. By 1973 the phase of rapid growth in keg beer sales had come to an end; however, sales of draught lager (which was in effect another variety of keg beer) simultaneously began to increase at an even faster rate (Table 3.2).

By the mid-1970s, therefore, keg beer in one form or another (bitter, lager and stout) accounted for about one third of total consumption, with lager being easily the most dynamic sector of the market. Just as the growth of bottled beer during the 1950s was commonly attributed to its popularity with younger drinkers, so the expansion of lager sales in the 1970s has been seen in much the same terms (Table 3.3).

Table 3.3   Beer drinkers' profile, 1973

	Bitter		Mild		Lager	
	% of drinkers	% of consumption	% of drinkers	% of consumption	% of drinkers	% of consumption
Sex						
Male	85	95	89	97	63	86
Female	15	5	11	3	37	14
Age						
16-34	44	47	30	32	67	75
35-44	17	17	20	23	15	12
45+	39	36	50	45	18	13
Social Group						
ABC_1	32	26	21	19	40	37
C_2DE	68	74	79	81	60	63

Source: *E. I. U. Retail Business* No. 266.

The market strength of lager, therefore, is based on its appeal to the young, to women and to middle and upper income groups.

Since the appeal of all forms of keg beer has become increasingly national in character and has transcended the traditional boundaries of local and regional preference, it is hardly surprising that the keg market has always been dominated by a small number of national brands. Moreover, keg beer can be transported in bulk for less than two thirds the cost of moving an equivalent amount of bottled beer, so that it can be produced and delivered to even the most remote public house relatively cheaply. In other words, keg beer is eminently suitable for production, advertising, marketing and distribution on a national scale. In 1972, for example, 82 per cent of keg bitter sales were accounted for by five national brands.[6] Similarly, in 1976 6 national brands together claimed 92 per cent of the lager market.[7] To some extent, of course, the dominance of national brands is simply a reflection of the rapid emergence of six major brewery groups during the 1960s, each owning a national chain of tied houses. In the early 1950s the national brewers supplied 25 per cent of total beer production; by the mid-1970s this proportion had risen to 70 per cent.[8] In 1952 the six largest brewers owned 16 per cent of the total number of public houses; by 1976 they owned 56 per cent.[9] But the dominance of national brands in the keg market was also due to the growing importance of the free trade from the early 1960s onwards.

In the early 1950s the free trade accounted for 25 per cent of total beer sales, the bulk of which was divided about equally between free public houses and clubs. The national brewers were strongly represented in the free trade through their branded bottled beers, some of which (as in the case of Ind Coope and Whitbread) were sold direct to free outlets and others (as with Bass and Guinness) were retailed through independent bottling firms. As a result, the free trade was a highly competitive business. Retail profit margins were relatively high, but wholesale margins were significantly lower than in the tied trade and price competition between the national and major regional brewers was frequently intense.[10] Indeed, many small and middle-sized brewery companies stood aloof from the free trade in the belief that it was hardly worth the effort.[11] The 1960s, however, witnessed a significant growth in the free trade so that in 1967 it accounted for 34 per cent of all beer sales, rising to 44 per cent by 1976.[12] This expansion was largely due to the Licensing Act of 1961, which removed certain restrictions on the growth of the off-licence sector. After 1961, it became increasingly rare for licensing justices to refuse an application for an off-licence simply on the grounds that a 'need' did not exist in the locality. The Act also enabled off-licences to remain open during normal shop hours. Before 1961, off-licences had to comply with the local 'permitted' hours, and multiple stores and supermarkets took the view that it would be more trouble than it was worth to have a separate off-licence section with its own peculiar trading hours. Two other expansionist influences were the Licensing Act of 1964, which made it much easier for restaurants to obtain liquor licences, and the abolition of Resale Price Maintenance in the same year which encouraged more supermarkets and specialist retailers to enter the field. Two additional sources of growth in the free trade were, firstly, a continuing increase in the number of registered clubs and, secondly, a growing tendency for brewery companies (especially the national groups) to sell off some of their less profitable houses to private entrepreneurs. Consequently between 1959 and 1975 the total number of licensed outlets increased by 24 per cent (from 126,000 to 156,000), with the main components of this growth being an increase in the number of registered clubs from 24,400 to 30,500, an increase in off-licences from 26,000 to 33,000 and the introduction of a new category of restricted licences (mainly for restaurants) which by 1975 applied to nearly 16,000 premises. By contrast, public houses continued to decline in number, from 75,500 in 1959 to barely 66,000 in 1975, although if all full on-licences are included the decline in this sector was rather less. The point to note, however, is that by the mid-1970s some 64 per cent of all licensed outlets, selling 44 per cent of beer sales by volume, were not under the ownership of brewery companies, in other words they were part of the free-trade.

The provisions of the Licensing Act of 1961 had an expansionist effect not only on the free trade in beer but also, and perhaps even more importantly, on the free trade in wines and spirits. The demand for cheap, branded table wines increased particularly rapidly during the late 1960s and early 1970s, reflecting another significant change in the pattern of British drinking habits (Table 3.4). In *per capita* terms the

Table 3.4   *Trends in drink consumption, 1945-75 (UK)*

Year	Beer (million b.b.)	Spirits (million proof gallons)	Heavy Wine (million proof gallons)	Table Wine (million proof gallons)
1945	31.0	8.3	4.4	
1950	25.8	9.8	11.6	
1955	23.6	11.5	16.9	
1960	26.6	14.2	16.8	10.2
1963	28.3	16.3	19.3	14.7
1965	29.9	19.1	20.2	16.2
1968	31.5	19.0	23.8	21.8
1970	33.5	18.0	24.4	24.0
1972	36.1	22.5	28.9	35.5
1975	38.5	20.7	30.9	46.6

Source: *E.I.U. Retail Business*, Nos. 192, 255.

broad trends were as shown in Table 3.5 opposite. These figures indicate that from the mid-1960s onwards, wines and spirits were both increasing their share of total expenditure on alcohol faster than beer. Thus in 1963 beer accounted for 60.7 per cent of total expenditure but over the next decade or so this proportion steadily fell, so that by

*Table 3.5 Alcohol consumption per head of population
aged 15 years and over, 1955-75 (pints)*

	1955	1960	1965	1970	1975
Beer	181.2	192.5	207.3	228.3	263.7
Spirits	3.1	3.9	5.1	4.7	8.7
Wine	3.4	4.7	7.1	8.1	14.9

Source: *E.I.U. Retail Business*, No. 225.

1976 wines and spirits absorbed half the market.[13] In 1973 table wines alone accounted for 8.5 per cent of total spending, the bulk of this going on cheap branded wines sold predominantly through specialist wine and spirit retailers and supermarkets.[14] The major brewery groups pioneered the introduction of these cheap branded wines in the late 1960s and dominated this section of the market thereafter. The strength of their position was partly attributable to the fact that they owned about 60 per cent of the specialist off-licences, but too much emphasis should not be placed on this advantage in view of the tendency for sales through non-specialist outlets, for example supermarkets, to increase at a much faster rate.

The rapid growth of the mass wine market was indicative of a major re-orientation of the major brewery groups towards the free trade. Even in the early 1970s wines and spirits accounted, on average, for less than 30 per cent of turnover in public houses, the balance of the market being in off-licences of various kinds. Success in the free trade required a strong wholesaling business which, in turn, meant that the brewers had to control leading brand names. Consequently, one important theme in the merger movement of the 1960s was the acquisition of hitherto independent wine and spirit wholesalers and shippers. Having acquired these brand names, and in some cases developed their own, the major brewers applied modern marketing techniques in order to build up their sales in the 'take-home' trade. The same strategy was adopted in respect of national brands of canned beer, which by 1975 accounted for nearly one third of the total consumption of 'packaged' beer. In short, the growth of the free trade in all forms of drink implied a radical change in the brewers' traditional approach to marketing. Surveying the industry in 1972, one stockbroking firm observed that: 'Drink is coming to be sold as a mass-market commodity, subject to the same sort of High Street selling pressure as washing powder and baked beans'.[15]

The Emergence of the National Brewery Groups

In the early 1950s the national brewers accounted for 25 per cent of beer output by value and about 18 per cent by volume. The adjective 'national' is to some extent misleading, however, since there were considerable differences between them in terms of organisation, production strategy and marketing arrangements. Only Guinness had truly national coverage in the sense that its single product — bottled stout — was obtainable in the vast majority of public houses and off-licences. As noted above, the company was not involved in retailing and relied on a national network of independent bottling firms, and in certain areas of high demand (such as Liverpool) on local breweries, to distribute its stout to the consumer. Bass and Worthington also relied on independent bottling firms, though to a lesser extent than Guinness in so far as they controlled a number of subsidiary companies. In addition the Bass group owned about 1,000 licensed houses and held 'umbrella' interests in a small number of brewery companies. In the free trade Bass relied mainly on its bottled brands, some of which were nationally known, though in its tied houses draught beer was more important. Whitbread bottled most of its own beer and sold it mainly through reciprocal trading arrangements with other national and regional companies and through its own 'umbrella' arrangements with local brewers. Whitbread's expansion through reciprocal trading, however, was limited by the fact that it owned only about 1,300 tied houses and showed no inclination to extend this coverage through direct acquisition.[16] Consequently during the 1950s the company persuaded those firms who went under its 'umbrella' to bottle its principal beers themselves.[17] The same strategy was applied to its major keg beer when the keg market began to expand in the following decade. At its fullest extent at the end of the 1950s the 'umbrella' gave Whitbread access to about 15,000 licensed houses covering much of the South, the South West, the Midlands, South Wales, West Yorkshire, Lancashire, the North East and parts of Scotland (Table 3.6). Ind Coope and Allsopp, by contrast, used direct acquisition to develop both its penetration of the free trade and its extensive reciprocal trading business. By 1960 the company owned about 5,200 licensed houses, which was more than all the other 'nationals' put together. Nevertheless, the bulk of its tied trade lay in the South and the Midlands and its coverage outside these areas depended on reciprocal trade with local breweries.[18] In the trade outside its own outlets, the company tended to concentrate on one brand of bottled beer, *Double Diamond,* which during the mid-1960s was increasingly sold in keg form. By 1961, when Ind Coope merged with

Table 3.6 Main brewery mergers and acquisitions 1955-72

1955 onwards	Establishment of the Whitbread 'umbrella' comprising some 20 local and regional companies. The majority of concerns were acquired outright in the 1960s, (see Table 3.9).
1956	John Courage merged with Barclay Perkins.
1958	Watney, Combe, Reid merged with Mann, Crossman and Paulin to form Watney Mann.
1959	Ind Coope acquired Taylor Walker.
	Formation of Northern Breweries of Great Britain – later renamed United Breweries – through the merger of Hope and Anchor Breweries, Hammond's United Breweries and John Jeffrey. Between 1960 and 1962 some 16 other concerns were acquired.
1960	Courage and Barclay merged with H. & G. Simonds to form Courage, Barclay and Simonds.
	Joshua Tetley merged with Walker Cain to form Tetley Walker.
	Scottish Breweries merged with Newcastle Breweries to form Scottish and Newcastle Breweries.
1961	Ind Coope, Tetley Walker and Ansell merged to form Ind Coope, Tetley, Ansell – later renamed Allied Breweries.
	Bass merged with Mitchells and Butlers.
	Courage, Barclay and Simonds acquired Bristol Brewery Georges.
1962	Charrington merged with United Breweries to form Charrington United Breweries.
1963	Allied Breweries acquired Friery Meux.
1966	Charrington acquired Massey's Burnley Brewery.
1967	Bass acquired Bent's Brewery.
	Bass merged with Charrington United Breweries to form Bass Charrington.
1970	Courage, Barclay and Simonds acquired John Smith's Tadcaster Brewery.
1971	Grand Metropolitan Hotels acquired Truman, Hanbury and Buxton.
1972	Grand Metropolitan Hotels acquired Watney Mann.
	Imperial Tobacco acquired Courage, Barclay and Simonds.

Tetley Walker and Ansell (to form Allied Breweries), reciprocal trading arrangements enabled the group's beers to be sold through 26,500 public houses and 5,600 off-licences.[19] Watney Combe Reid had the least-developed coverage as a national company in the early 1950s. Its tied trade was based firmly in London and the Home Counties and up to 1959 those acquisitions it made (Tamplin's of Brighton in 1954 and Henty and Constable of Chichester in 1955) merely strengthened and extended its regional coverage. Its strategy in the free trade in the southern counties was based on direct bottling and selling through its own depots; elsewhere it relied on independent bottling firms to whom it sent beer in bulk.[20] Despite these differences between the national brewers, however, they all had one characteristic in common, namely a growing determination to penetrate each other's outlets, to sell their main brands through the houses of the smaller brewers, and to increase their share of the free trade.

The same could also be said of at least some of the regional companies who, by the early 1950s, constituted a very significant force within the industry. Vaizey included in this category all those firms who brewed over 200,000 barrels a year and owned between 300 and 1,000 licensed houses. Using these criteria, he estimated that there were between 30 and 40 regional companies in the UK, none of whom, however, had a monopoly in their own region. 'In every region there is an oligopolistic situation where large brewers of comparable (but not necessarily equal) size compete'.[21] These regional firms were, of course, based on a long series of mergers and acquisitions involving small local breweries, and in some areas the process of concentration had reached a more advanced stage than in others. In the London and Birmingham areas, for example, most of the smaller firms had disappeared during the interwar years; in Lancashire and the West Riding, by contrast, small breweries survived in relatively large numbers. Against a background of declining demand, a company operating in a relatively concentrated market could only grow either by merging with one of its major competitors or, alternatively, by acquiring smaller breweries with trading interests in adjacent regions. Thus both Mitchells and Butlers and Ansell moved into South Wales by acquiring respectively Thatcher's Brewery and Lloyds (both of Newport) in 1951. In similar fashion, Charrington sought to break out of their east London base by acquiring Thompson's of Deal (Kent) in 1951, the Kemp Town Brewery (Brighton) in 1954 and Brutton Mitchell Toms (Somerset) in 1959. Simultaneously two regional companies in the north east — Vaux and Cameron — extended their interests into Scotland and Yorkshire respectively.[22] Where the opportunities for small-scale, piecemeal expansion were more limited, mergers between companies of roughly equal size were more common. Thus in 1956 Courage merged with Barclay Perkins to form one of the biggest groups in the London area and then linked up with the West Country brewer, H. and G. Simonds. Other major developments in the London area included the merger of Meux with Friary Holroyd and Healey's Brewery (Guildford) in 1956 and, on a larger scale, the amalgamation of Watney, Combe, Reid with Mann, Crossman and Paulin in 1958.[23] In 1956 Cheltenham and Hereford Breweries merged with the Stroud Brewery to form West Country Brewery Holdings Ltd. In Bristol, the two remaining independent firms (Bristol Georges and Bristol United Breweries) merged, which gave the new company a virtual monopoly of the city's licensed trade. In Birmingham, Ansell, and Mitchells and Butlers seriously considered joining forces but the proposed merger never materialised.[24] By contrast, in other areas where the market was still relatively fragmented, some companies strengthened their regional status by acquiring small (usually family-owned) breweries as and when they became available. Firms in this category included Hammond's United Breweries (Bradford), Greenall Whitley (Warrington), J. W. Green (Luton, subsequently Flowers Breweries), Tennant Bros. (Sheffield), Tetley (Leeds) and H. & G. Simonds (Reading).[25] The larger regional firms, particularly Ansell, Charrington and Courage Barclay, were increasingly aware of the need to expand in the regional free trade, and acquisitions of tied outlets were often used as a springboard from which to penetrate this section of the market. Other firms, however, concentrated primarily on expanding their tied trade as an end in itself, although this did not exclude the acquisition of wine and spirit and mineral water businesses.[26]

What were the reasons behind these mergers? One obvious factor which has already been touched upon, and which was particularly influential during the inter-war period, was the declining level of demand for beer during the post-war decade. As Vaizey observed in the late 1950s:

> The fall in the demand for draught beer which has been the predominant trend for fifty years has made fixed expenses a frequent preoccupation to most firms. Not only is fixed equipment extremely durable, but it also is made up of a large number of different items, each of which has to be replaced at different intervals. Firms do not shrink, they simply have idle capacity and they continue to replace equipment so long as the total return constitutes sufficient profits on the one item to justify its replacement. There is thus a persistent tendency for excess capacity to remain in the industry, and a persistent incentive to maintain or expand sales.[27]

The continued expansion of the bottled beer trade up to the late 1950s placed many smaller firms at a disadvantage since bottling plant was relatively expensive to acquire and the market was in any case dominated by the national and regional brewers. Furthermore, the continued exodus of population from the major urban centres to the suburbs and beyond gave the large metropolitan brewers a strong incentive to spread their tied trade more widely. The small 'inner city' brewer, by contrast, often lacked the resources to break out of his market and was therefore compelled either to sell out or simply watch his trade and his outlets being eroded away.[28] The small, family-dominated concern also faced the perennial problems of financing death duties and providing sufficient male heirs to ensure continuity of control. None of these factors were new to the brewing industry of the 1950s. Consequently the character of merger activity retained its traditional features. Mergers were usually arranged through personal friendships or family connexions; third parties did not intervene in negotiations between buyer and seller; post-merger rationalisation was often slow, and proceeded with due regard to the paternalist traditions of the industry.[29] The rate of merger activity was therefore restricted by the supply of available businesses and at the end of the 1950s brewing was still one of the least concentrated manufacturing industries.[30]

From 1959 onwards, however, the rate of concentration began to accelerate rapidly as more and more firms of all sizes became involved in mergers. Kuehn, for example, has estimated that 59 per cent of the 166 companies in the industry were absorbed by mergers during the period 1957-69, a proportion which was surpassed (and then only narrowly) by one other industry — soft drinks.[31] The process of concentration continued into the early 1970s, though at a declining rate, so that by 1976 only 77 brewery companies were still in operation. A more accurate impression, however, may be gained from Table 3.7.

Table 3.7 Concentration ratios in the brewing industry, 1954-68

	The five largest enterprise's percentage share of the total for the industry			
	1954 %	1958 %	1963 %	1968 %
Net output	18	23	42	64
Employment	19	22	49	61
Purchase of materials and goods	23	23	43	52
Plant and machinery installed	21	32	33	63

Source: *Censuses of Production* 1954-68.

It must be emphasised, however, that even in 1968 the concentration ratio in brewing was still slightly below the average for manufacturing industry as a whole. There were 185 product groups with a higher ratio than brewing and 148 with a lower one, leaving an average of 65 per cent.[32] Nevertheless it is clear that while twelve years of intense merger activity (an experience shared by many other industries) did not result in an exceptional degree of horizontal integration in brewing, it certainly brought the industry much closer to the national average. Of the 98 mergers and acquisitions which took place in the industry, no fewer than 35 occurred in the three-year period 1959-61. This in itself is significant in so far as there was no comparable merger boom in this short period in any other major manufacturing industry. In other industries the most intensive phase of concentration occurred in 1967-69, when the brewery sector was less active. Why, then, did the industry witness so many mergers in the earlier period?

The boom of 1959-61 was occasioned partly by the introduction of a new factor into brewing mergers, namely the growing realisation in the City that the industry's major asset — licensed property — was undervalued and underutilised. The first indication that this fact was becoming known to the financial world at large came in 1955, when a large financial group attempted to acquire Cheltenham and Hereford Breweries Ltd. In March 1955 the company's properties were independently valued at £4.47 million against a book value of £1.6 million, indicating a large hidden reserve and considerable scope for further development. The attempt to acquire the company was in the event defeated by the intervention of Whitbread, which took an 'umbrella' holding in the equity. Yet the episode conveyed a clear warning to the rest of the industry, as Col. Whitbread himself admitted:

> A well-managed company like the Cheltenham and Hereford Breweries has a local tradition and is a human entity with staff and employees who have worked with the company for many years and their fathers, and grandfathers in some cases, before them; they may also hope that their sons will be employed in the organisation. It seems to me that a company such as this, with all its staff and employees, is of great human importance and it would not be in the best interests of the brewing industry, or indeed of the country, for such an entity to be liquidated for the benefit of a quick profit for purely financial interests . . . The moral of this story seems to be that a company which has run its finances in the most conservative manner, ploughing back a large proportion of its profits into the business, may lay itself open to financial marauders who plan to liquidate it and sell its assets with complete disregard for those who work in the company . . . I am convinced that the continuance of old-established concerns, run on progressive lines, is in the public interest and consequently sound business. It is this conviction that lies behind our policy of cooperating with sound concerns by providing them with both financial and commercial assistance and thus enabling them to continue as individual entities.[33]

Here indeed was the authentic voice of tradition. The root of the problem, however, was that tradition could not be preserved without a major effort within the industry to increase the return on its assets — a strategy which might in itself destroy the tradition it was intended to uphold.

The discrepancy between the existing and alternative use values of licensed property, and the generally depressed share prices of brewery companies during the 1950s, attracted the attention of a much more powerful 'financial marauder' in the shape of Charles Clore, chairman of Sears Holdings Ltd. Clore was an entrepreneur with a special interest in 'development situations' and had played a major role in the property boom in London during the 1950s. In 1959 Sears Holdings launched a take-over bid for Watney Mann, which since its formation the previous year had become the largest single brewery company in London and the home counties, owning 3,900 licensed houses. Clore bid a cash equivalent of 60s. for the 9 million Watney ordinary shares compared with a pre-bid price of 51s. 3d. This valued Watney's ordinary capital at £27 million, while its net book assets stood at £37.8 million. Clore indicated that it was his intention to 'dynamicise' the management of Watney's property assets and thereby increase their profitability. He was particularly anxious to increase the turnover of the company's prime-site public houses through modernisation and the provision of a wider range of amenities, while 'uneconomic' outlets were to be sold or redeveloped. As *The Economist* observed at the time: '. . . Clore is not offering anything new . . . his recipe amounts to rather more of what the trade has been trying in its own plodding pace to do for some years in order to offset the declining trend in beer consumption'.[34] Over the period 1955-59 Watney had in fact closed 150 'uneconomic' public houses and sold a further 18. Clore clearly believed, however, that with a more aggressive, professional approach to property management, much more progress could be made. In the event the bid was defeated not so much by the determined opposition of the Watney Mann directors but by the fact that in anticipation of a second and higher offer from Clore, buyers had forced the price of Watney's equity up to a level which Clore considered unrealistic. He was not, he said, prepared '. . . to pay a price which discounts the future too fully and which does not take into account the time and effort which will be necessary before the future benefits accrue'.[35] The lesson was not lost on Watney Mann, however, which immediately initiated a programme of defensive mergers on a national scale. The company moved into the North West (Wilson and Walker of Manchester, 1959), the West Country (Usher's of Trowbridge, 1960), East Anglia (Morgans, 1961; Steward and Patteson, 1963; Bullards, 1963), the Midlands (Phipps of Northampton, 1960) and Scotland (Dryborough of Edinburgh, 1965). These acquisitions added a further 3,000 licensed houses to Watney's tied estate and gave the company a national status. They did not in themselves, however, provide the group with a secure with which senior management set about the problem of improving the return on their assets.

The financial theory of mergers postulates that an acquisition will take place if the valuation placed on a company by a potential acquirer is greater than the valuation placed on it by the existing owners and if the discounted stream of expected profits satisfies normal investment appraisal criteria. If one looks, for example, at several brewery companies who went under the Whitbread 'umbrella' (and were mostly absorbed by Whitbread during the 1960s), the persistent under-valuation of assets is emphasised (Table 3.8). As Whitbread directors were present on the boards of almost all these companies for several years prior to formal mergers being agreed, it must be assumed that the former were in a position to acquaint themselves in some detail with the earnings potential of these firms. Whitbread however, were unique in this respect. Many small and middle-sized companies were acquired by the emerging national groups within a short period of time before any real investment appraisal could be carried out. The dangers involved were obvious. As one major brewery chairman pointed out: 'If one buys on what looks like a reasonable earnings yield and then has to improve both beer and pubs, that reasonable earnings yield can become a very unreasonable loss.'[36] Another difficulty was that when the merger boom began to subside from 1962 onwards, it became a relatively simple matter for the speculative investor to pick out those firms which were likely to be absorbed by one of the national groups. Consequently the stock market tended to up-value the equity of vulnerable firms (especially those which were known to be under a major group's 'umbrella') and this tended to reduce their earnings yield. In the few situations where competitive bidding developed, the final price was largely a function of the determination of the parties concerned. In the battle between Courage Barclay Simonds and United Breweries for control of Bristol Brewery Georges (1961), for example, the successful offer from Courage valued the firm at nearly £18 millions compared with a pre-bid market capitalisation of £11 millions. If United's second offer had been accepted, it would in effect have nearly doubled Bristol's pre-bid value. In defence of the active bidders, however, it could be argued that many offers appeared more generous than they were because of the major discrepancies between the book asset value per share of acquired firms and their real market value. The offer which United Breweries made for the Cornbrook Brewery Co. Ltd. in 1961, for example, valued the latter's ordinary shares at 153s. compared with a pre-bid market price of 145s. These terms seemed generous in view of

Table 3.8 The Whitbread 'umbrella' in 1962: valuation of assets

Company	Share price[a]		Asset value per share	Book value of properties (£m)	Last valued	Number of properties	Average book value per property (£)	Asset value on 100% apprec. of property value
Bentley's Yorkshire Breweries	(5s)	48s	17s 6d	2.02	1947	420	4,800	42s 3d
Brickwood	(£1)	90s	50s 6d	5.59	1947	850	6,600	98s 0d
Dutton's Blackburn	(5s)	18s	13s 7d	8.33	1954	820	10,200	22s 9d
Flowers	(5s)	24s	14s 0d	12.87	1960	1,125	11,400	15s 6d
Fremlin	(£1)	120s	46s 6d	4.65	1949	920	5,000	123s 0d
Lacon	(£1)	62s	30s 0d	1.31	1947	410	3,200	64s 6d
Marston	(5s)	21s	11s 0d	2.38	1947	900	2,650	19s 6d
Morland	(£1)	85s	51s 6d	1.07	1941	290	3,700	108s 6d
Rhymney	(£1)	120s	64s 0d	4.05	1948	680	6,000	150s 6d
Starkey Knight	(£1)	150s	44s 9d	1.17	1947	450	2,600	199s 6d
Strong	(5s)	50s	15s 6d	5.15	1938	750	6,900	47s 9d
West Country	(£1)	110s	36s 0d	3.41	1947	1,250	2,750	77s 0d

Source: *Stock Exchange Gazette*, 4 May 1962.
[a] as at 4 May 1962.

the fact that Cornbrook's assets stood in the 1960 balance sheet at only 60s. a share, except that the assets (mainly licensed property) had not been revalued since 1947. Investment analysts who reviewed brewery balance sheets at the end of the 1950s tended to add anything between 80 per cent and 100 per cent to the book value of their assets, which usually raised their market value to a level significantly in excess of their current market price.[37] In this sense it would be misleading to conclude that in the course of the merger boom the national groups in general paid too much for their acquisitions. Even the most generous offer must be seen as an investment in an appreciating and under-used asset, namely licensed property.

Asset-inflation due to competitive bidding was, however, exceptional. Many mergers were in fact initiated by the 'victim' company in circumstances which effectively precluded unwelcome intervention by a third party. The mere possibility of a bid from an unwelcome quarter was often sufficient to induce the directors of small and middle-sized firms to approach an 'acceptable' company for protection. Such approaches were invariably made in the greatest secrecy and, if successful, would be presented to the company's shareholders as a *fait accompli*. In cases where the initiative came from the bidding company, the same secrecy was normally preserved. The purpose was, of course, to conclude merger terms before any other group could intervene with a counter-bid. The main result was that the shareholders of many acquired firms did not make the capital gains which they might have done if competitive bidding had been more widespread. Indeed, at least one company was acquired for a price which almost certainly under-valued its assets.[38] To this extent, the traditional norms of the brewing industry were preserved, even at the height of the merger boom. Yet the very fact that most acquisitions were arranged along these lines suggests that a purely financial theory of merger activity was no more applicable to the brewing industry during this period of rapid concentration than it had been before. The merger boom of 1959-61 was fundamentally defensive in character. Many acquisitions were inspired by the victim firm's fear of either being left out in the cold or compelled to join a group which for some reason was not acceptable. Consequently the role of traditional friendships and personal antipathies was of immense significance in determining many individual merger decisions, with objective financial considerations being relegated to a position of relatively minor importance.

One of the most important influences in this field was the ambitions and activities of a Canadian entrepreneur named E. P. Taylor and of the group which he was instrumental in forming — United Breweries. Between 1934 and 1954 Taylor had built up his own company, Canadian Breweries, through a series of rapid mergers to the point where it supplied over half the total output of beer in the provinces of Quebec and Ontario. During the 1950s Taylor was also expanding his interests in the USA through a subsidiary company, Carling Breweries Inc. Taylor's interest in the British brewing industry sprang from his desire to develop the European market for *Carling* lager (his company's leading beer) and, more generally, from his conviction that the industry itself was 'ripe for rationalisation'. From 1953 onwards, *Carling* was brewed, bottled and sold in the UK on Taylor's behalf by Hope and Anchor Breweries Ltd.[39] By 1958, however, Hope and Anchor's limitations as a trading partner were becoming all too clear. The only way in which *Carling* could achieve significant penetration of the UK market was through the tied house system, and with barely 150 houses Hope and Anchor's tied trade was clearly inadequate for this purpose. Taylor therefore agreed to buy a large minority holding in Hope and Anchor and proceeded to use this as a stepping stone towards the formation of a national brewing group in the UK. Over the next two years he succeeded in persuading Hammond's United Breweries, Cornbrook, Caterall and Swarbrick, Hewitt Bros. and a number of smaller firms to join his group which, trading under the name of United Breweries, comprised a chain of 2,800 houses by the end of 1961.

Taylor also extended his interests in Scotland. The Scottish brewing industry was, to an even greater extent than in England, dominated by family firms. Prior to 1939 many of them had relied on a flourishing world-wide export trade in lager and pale ale. In the post-war years, however, this export trade had rapidly declined as former colonial customers began to develop their own brewing industries behind high tariff walls. This left the Scottish brewers with no option but to compete in their own stagnant domestic market. This situation called for a considerable degree of rationalisation yet, despite the weakness in Scotland of the tied house system, the process of concentration was generally slow during the 1950s. The main stumbling block was the reluctance of many family firms to lose their identity and see their beers and breweries disappear. The growth of competition in the home market prompted some companies to break with tradition and integrate forward into the retail trade either by the loan tie or by the purchase of licensed houses.[40] The consequent rise in the value of licensed property, however, made forward integration an expensive method of growth, leaving many firms unable to improve their houses once they had acquired them or, equally important, to modernise their production plant.[41] The exception to this general rule was Scottish Breweries Ltd., formed in 1931 from a merger of William Younger and William McEwan. In 1960, Scottish Brewers merged with the Newcastle Breweries Ltd. to form Scottish and Newcastle Breweries and the new group continued to strengthen its position in Scotland through further acquisitions. Consequently when Taylor opened negotiations with the directors of several Scottish firms in 1960 there was a growing feeling that mergers were more or less inevitable. Nevertheless, it appears that Taylor had a catalytic effect on these companies, and in the course of 1960 five of them joined the United Breweries group.[42]

The significance of Taylor's activities, however, also lay in the effect which he had on the directors of companies who did not join his group. His open, direct approach violated the tradition that mergers should be decided by long-maturing personal friendships and family connexions. His public image was that of a brash, Canadian entrepreneur and that in itself was sufficient to induce several of his prospective acquisitions to seek protection elsewhere. Having secured a strong base in Yorkshire, Taylor was particularly anxious to strengthen his interests in Lancashire and approached Walker Cain Ltd. with a view to their joining United Breweries. Walker Cain responded by merging with Tetley, thereby forming a northern regional group of comparable size to United Breweries. Taylor also wanted to expand into Wales, and approached the chairman of William Hancock & Co. Ltd., the largest independent company in South Wales with over 600 houses. Hancock immediately asked Bass to buy an 'umbrella' holding in their equity.[43] Early in 1961 he turned his attention to Bristol Brewery Georges & Co. Ltd., one of the few surviving medium-sized companies in the west country which was not under the Whitbread 'umbrella'. The Bristol board rejected United's offer and quickly accepted a higher bid from Courage Barclay Simonds Ltd., which was equally anxious to consolidate its position in the West Country. Despite a second and higher offer from United, the Bristol board's support for the Courage offer was decisive.[44] Shortly afterwards, Ind Coope merged with Ansell and Tetley Walker to form what was then easily the biggest national group in the UK, with 9,500 licensed houses and a market capitalisation of £126 millions. A correspondent in *The Times* observed that the major reason for this triple link-up was clearly defensive, and suggested that it was directed against Taylor.[45] This merger clearly showed, however, that Taylor was not alone in his belief that national groups and national brands held the key to the future growth of the brewing industry. It also underlined an important weakness in Taylor's strategy. Most of the major regional companies refused to merge with United Breweries, forcing him to concentrate on smaller local firms. Yet, as the formation of Ind Coope Tetley Ansell demonstrated, the logical basis for a national group was a merger between large regional or quasi-national firms with well-established brand names in their product portfolios. Indeed, it was precisely on this basis that Bass merged with Mitchells and Butlers a few months later. Until 1962, however, when Charrington & Co. Ltd. was persuaded to merge with United Breweries, Taylor only succeeded in acquiring small breweries whose beers were hardly known outside their immediate trading areas.

The opposition to Taylor was fundamentally irrational in character, and the relatively generous offers he made were often insufficient to overcome the widespread distrust evoked by his brash, 'transatlantic' style. In June 1960, for example, he admitted that in recent weeks no fewer than five brewery companies to whom he had made approaches had in fact joined other groups without giving adequate consideration to his own proposals: 'The price they got for their shareholders was below what we were prepared to offer', he observed.[46] The battle for Bristol Georges, however, was interpreted in the financial press as indicative of the determination of the 'traditionalists' in the industry to frustrate Taylor's ambitions at almost any price. Commenting on the counter-offer by Courage for the Bristol firm, one financial journalist argued:

> At last the brewery 'establishment' has reacted violently to the rapid expansion of United Breweries under the leadership of that thrusting Canadian, Mr E. P. Taylor . . . What is it that has added nearly £7 millions to the value of this excellent West Country brewery in a matter of only a few weeks? Almost certainly this rise stems solely from Mr Taylor's determination to make United Breweries into as powerful a force in this country as his Canadian Breweries is in the USA and Canada. And now, it would seem, the establishment has decided to oppose this expansion.[47]

In the aftermath of the Bristol battle, Taylor sought to calm the hostility towards his company in general and himself in particular:

> United has never been an 'invader' but instead tries to bring companies together for their mutual advantage . . . United's announced policy is not to make acquisition proposals against the wishes of boards of directors, unless it has evidence that offers are forthcoming from other sources. United has no reason to believe that any consortium of brewers is operating against it or that a large section of the trade is unfriendly to it.[48]

He repeatedly emphasised that any companies he acquired would continue to operate as semi-independent concerns: 'I want local autonomy, with separate boards for the operating companies who join the family and I would not change the firm's name on a pub.[49] These were hardly the words of a man who was intent on rationalising his acquisitions and exploiting all opportunities to make economies of scale. In fact Taylor's overriding interest was in the process of acquisition *per se* and he took little interst in the subsequent management of his acquisitions. United Breweries' management structure reflected Taylor's approach in so far as it was extremely decentralised. Regional management companies were formed in Yorkshire, Lancashire and Scotland which, at least in the first two cases, merely co-ordinated the policies of the constituent companies and eliminated unnecessary duplication. Otherwise, these companies retained their own names, their own products and their own boards of directors.[50]

To some extent, of course, this philosophy of decentralisation simply reflected the haphazard, opportunistic nature of United Breweries' expansion. Although by the end of 1961 United owned 2,800 licensed houses, these were distributed between 15 companies scattered over a wide area from Wales to Scotland. It was clear to the board, therefore, that if United was to achieve anything approaching national status it would have to merge with another major group with strong tied trade interests in at least some of the areas where United had no representation. Charrington & Co. Ltd. was in many ways an appropriate partner. Over the preceding decade Charrington had succeeded in breaking out of their traditional base in east London into Kent, Sussex, Surrey and the West Country. The remaining opportunities for making small acquisitions in the southern counties, however, were rapidly disappearing as Whitbread, Watney Mann and Courage all extended and consolidated their trade in the south and west. Moreover, the speculative rise in the market value of brewery shares which began in 1950 effectively ruled out a major acquisition by Charrington. In the words of one former director 'We concluded that Charrington's financial rating in the City was not high enough for anyone to have underwritten a big issue of shares if we had wanted to make a further acquisition'. Like all the other major London breweries, Charrington's property assets were considerably undervalued and the real rate of return was correspondingly lower than the modest 3-4 per cent indicated by the balance sheet. Moreover, its share-ownership was widely spread and the family holdings would have provided no defence against an unwelcome bid. A merger with United Breweries would therefore give some protection while simultaneously preserving Charrington's regional autonomy. As the chairman of Charrington United Breweries told the new group's share-holders at their first annual meeting in 1962:

> Some brewery mergers are brought about because additional profits can be seen for the resulting combine through economies which can be made in production and distribution. Others are indicated by the difficulties in which local concerns find themselves when confronted with competition from larger ones, or through the incidence of death duties in family businesses. Others yet again are combined of firms whose interests are so diverse that virtually no competition exists between them, either geographically or through the similarity of their products, but who see benefits resulting from a widening of the sale of their advertised brands by a greatly increased number of outlets. This is the category into which our merger falls . . ..

Nevertheless, Taylor's lack of success in persuading other companies to join United Breweries in its formative years had a more long-term result in so far as it left Charrington United Breweries without any real coverage in the midlands and with only a few scattered outlets in certain other areas. In the mid-1960s it was still axiomatic that the marketing of national brands required nation-wide representation in the tied trade. This geographical weakness ultimately played an important role in Charrington United Breweries' decision to merge with Bass Mitchells and Butlers in 1967.

The search for economies in production and distribution was a stronger motive behind the merger of Bass with Mitchells and Butlers (1961) than it was in the formation of Charrington United Breweries. Yet here again, defensive factors appear to have played a dominant role in determining the merger. This was particularly true of Bass, for by the end of the 1950s, Bass's trade was undoubtedly declining. For many years the company's strength in the free trade (and in the 1950s approximately 70 per cent of its total output was still sold through either free outlets or other brewers' houses) had relied on the willingness of local and regional firms to sell bottled Bass and Worthington as their 'national' beers. To a great extent, however, the security of this trade reflected the relative absence of real opposition in the 'national' sector of the market. During the postwar period this situation changed quite dramatically as Ind Coope and Whitbread both adopted a more aggressive approach to the free-trade. Both these companies were also actively extending their reciprocal trade with local firms and these arrangements frequently excluded Bass. As mergers proceeded in the 1950s, Bass found its trade in the small brewery sector subject to further attrition as some of its traditional customers were absorbed by larger firms who were anxious to develop their own bottled beer trade. Bass's tied trade was too small and its licensed houses in too poor a condition to compensate the company for its declining competitiveness in the free trade.[51] In theory, of course, Bass could easily have imitated Whitbread's strategy and built up a national network of 'umbrella' holdings in order to protect its trade. In practice, however, the Bass directors were overwhelmingly complacent about their company's position, believing that other brewers would be compelled to continue selling their beers simply due to the pressure of public demand. Such 'umbrella' holdings as they had proved to be an inadequate defence against a determined bidder and they made no move to counteract these bids.[52] By 1959 the board had reconciled themselves to the inevitability of a merger and tentative discussions had begun with Watney Mann, leading to an exchange of directors. The negotiations foundered, however, on the question of who was to be chairman of the new group and on the acquisition by Watney Mann of Wilson and Walker, in which Bass had an 'umbrella' holding. But the removal of Watney Mann as a potential partner did not remove Bass's need to merge with a company which had a more professional, forward-looking management and a strong base in tied trade.

In many ways Mitchells and Butlers were well-suited to be a partner for Bass. Since the appointment of H. Alan Walker as chief executive in 1956, the company had acquired a strong reputation for efficiency and professionalism. Within three years of his appointment he had increased the company's output by nearly one third and reduced the labour force by 800. The increase in output was achieved partly by a determined push into the free trade in Birmingham, hitherto dominated by Ansell, and by 1960 this sector absorbed 30 per cent of the company's output (compared with 17 per cent in 1956). It was also achieved by the acquisition in 1959 of Atkinson's Brewery Ltd., a family-dominated firm with 360 houses in the West Midlands and a brewery producing 150,000 barrels a year (which was closed after the merger). Shortly after the Atkinson merger the company's regional coverage was greatly strengthened by the acquisition of W. Butler & Co. Ltd. of Wolverhampton, which had 830 houses spread over a wide area within the west midlands.[53] The problem was, however, that the company was still essentially regional, and by 1961 it was clear that the brewing industry would sooner or later be dominated by a small number of national groups. Walker realised therefore that unless he took the initative and merged with a company of his own choice, Mitchells and Butlers might well find itself under attack from a bigger group. Bass was regarded as a suitable match for three reasons: firstly, its leading brand names were nationally known; secondly, it had a national distribution network; and thirdly, it had large financial reserves. Walker therefore approached Sir James Grigg, the recently-appointed chairman of Bass, and suggested a merger. The normal argument over who should be chairman of the new group — a rock on which several proposed mergers foundered — was avoided by an agreement that Grigg would retain the chairmanship and Walker would become the chief executive.

In 1967 Bass, Mitchells and Butlers merged with Charrington United Breweries to establish the largest brewing concern in the country with over 11,000 outlets. This merger can be viewed as a logical culmination of the process of national expansion begun with the earlier mergers of Bass with Mitchells and Butlers, and Charrington with United Breweries. It gave Charrington a strong tied house base in the one area where it was weak — the Midlands, but more importantly, product-wise, it gave the company what it was previously lacking — well known national brands of beer. For Bass the importance of the merger lay in the fact that it give the company a significant national presence in the tied trade and provided a new impetus to its position in the free trade, both areas in which its sales were being increasingly threatened by competition from Allied and Whitbread.

The merger boom clearly demonstrated that an 'umbrella' holding of, say, 15-30 per cent in a company's equity was an inadequate defence against a determined third party. In 1959 Bass saw Wilson and Walker fall to Watney Mann, and over the next two years Whitbread lost two of its 'umbrella' companies (Hewitt Bros. and Wells and Winch) to other bidders. This experience induced the Whitbread board to discontinue its 'umbrella' strategy and adopt a programme of direct acquisitions. This programme was implemented from 1961 onwards (Table 3.9).

Even when this programme had been completed, Whitbread still retained minority holdings in Truman, Boddington, Border Breweries, Buckley, Devenish, Marston, Morland and Brickwood. However, only one of these companies — Brickwood — was subsequently absorbed into the group, and it is clear that by 1970 the Whitbread board took the view that the group had achieved sufficient national coverage in terms of tied trade. Whitbread was the only national group which emerged without the acquisition of a company of comparable size; its purchases were exclusively concentrated among middle-sized and small firms. This underlines the significance of the 'umbrella' strategy developed in the post-war period. Far more than any of the other national brewers, Whitbread reinforced its reciprocal trading agreements with equity holdings and in the 1960s the strategy readily facilitated the company's

Table 3.9 *The growth of Whitbread & Co. Ltd., 1961-69*

Company	Trading area	Number of properties	Year of acquisition
Tennant Bros.	S. Yorkshire	N/A	1961
Norman and Pring	Devon	N/A	1961
West Country Breweries	Wales and West	1,250	1962
Flower	Midlands	1,125	1962
Starkey Knight	South West	450	1962
Dutton's Blackburn	Lancashire	820	1963
J. Nimmo	North East	150	1963
Rhymney Breweries	Wales	680	1966
Evans Evans Bevan	Wales	300	1967
Archibald Campbell	Scotland	N/A	1967
Threlfalls Chesters	North West	800	1967
E. Lacon	E. Anglia	410	1967
Fremlin	Kent	920	1968
Bentley	Yorkshire	200	1968
Richard Whitaker	Yorkshire	200	1968
Strong & Co.	South	750	1969

Source: *Brewing Trade Review*, various issues.

growth through acquisition. Once the company had demonstrated its intention of absorbing its 'umbrella' partners, other groups declined to intervene when the formal offers were eventually made. The only exception was the bid which Allied Breweries made for Boddington in 1969. Whitbread's response was to use its 'umbrella' holding to support the Boddington family (which also held a significant minority of the shares) and the combination was sufficient to preserve the company's independence. Whitbread's acquisition strategy, therefore, was essentially defensive. It did not begin to purchase its trading partners outright until its national competitors began to acquire similar companies, thereby threatening the safety of the 'umbrella'.

To summarise, the period of rapid concentration which began in 1959 and more or less came to an end in 1968 was dominated by a mixture of expansionist and defensive objectives. The Clore bid for Watney Mann was a clear warning to the industry as a whole that it would have to take action to improve the return on its property assets. In practical terms this meant that a much more 'commercial' attitude would have to be adopted towards the management of tied houses, and widespread mergers were of critical importance in facilitating this normative change. This point is analysed in more detail below. It is certainly true, therefore, that many acquisitions 'were made with an eye on undervalued tied estates, and with the confidence that the over-all rate of return on capital could be raised'.[54] It would also be correct to say that given the growing importance of national brands of beer (especially keg beer), and the fact that the overall level of demand was rising slowly, aspiring national firms could only expand rapidly through the acquisition of tied outlets and distribution areas. In the market environment of the 1960s, the logic of 'going national' was unanswerable. On the other hand specific merger decisions were frequently influenced by personal and political factors which in effect precluded rational cost-benefit analysis. If one theme in the merger boom was the desire to avoid being acquired by a bidder from outside the brewing industry, another and perhaps even more influential factor was the fear of being absorbed by an 'undesirable' group within the industry. The activities of E. P. Taylor and United Breweries were thus of immense significance in shaping the composition of the major groups which emerged from the boom of the early 1960s. The strong defensive theme in the merger boom had important implications both for the nature of competition in the industry and for the subsequent attempts of the national groups to improve the return on their assets. These will now be analysed.

4 Market Structure and Competition

Mergers, Vertical Integration and Competition

The rapid concentration of the brewing industry during the 1960s was entirely the result of a series of horizontal mergers, which by 1968 had left the seven largest companies with 73 per cent of total beer production in the UK. Since 1968 the leading companies have increased their market share further, partly by acquisition of smaller concerns but more importantly by greater penetration in the free trade (Table 4.1).

Table 4.1 Beer market shares, 1976

Company	Number of UK breweries	Share of beer sales %
Bass Charrington	12	20
Allied Breweries	7	17
Whitbread	19	13
Watney/Grand Metropolitan Hotels	8	12
Scottish & Newcastle	3	11
Courage/Imperial Group	8	9
Guinness	1	9
Others	89	9
Total	147	100

Source: Brewers Society and Economist Intelligence Unit estimates.

This degree of horizontal integration was regarded with considerable suspicion by the Price Commission (1977):

> When one looks not at the detail but at the picture as a whole, the most striking point is the degree of horizontal and vertical integration in the industry. Horizontally, the industry is dominated by six concerns who over the years have pursued an aggressive policy of amalgamation and acquisition. Vertically, it is highly integrated from the brewery to the public house. . . . Not only is brewing a highly concentrated industry, but there are significant barriers to entry and virtually no competition from imports.

These are the classic conditions for a monopoly which is likely to operate to the detriment of consumers. Legislation over a long period of time has undoubtedly contributed to the present situation. Nevertheless, the simple truth is that the way this trade is organised and run has a profound effect on prices and profits. The question which has to be asked is whether the present situation is contrary to the public interest.[1]

An earlier investigation by the Monopolies Commission (1969) curiously enough failed to discuss the implications of horizontal integration and concentrated almost exclusively on vertical integration. The Commission's critique of the system suggested that it had hindered the entry of new producers and new products into the industry, that it had weakened or prevented the growth of independent wholesalers of wines and spirits, and that it had greatly reduced the force of competition in the retail trade. This last point was in fact the kernel of the Commission's case:

> . . . competition among brewers principally takes the form of competition to acquire captive portions of the retail market and to improve the amenities of their captive outlets; as a result the retail trade is generally more uncompetitive than it would be in any event in conditions of restrictive licensing; and, in particular, in the on-licensed retail trade price competition is practically absent and licensees tend to conform to a type which is content to avoid active competition.[2]

The Commission also alleged that the tied house system had retarded both the elimination of inefficient and redundant production capacity and the development of 'rational' systems of distribution. The statements quoted above add up to a strong attack on the tied house system. Indeed, the Commission openly declared that in their view '. . . a state of affairs in which brewers did not own or control licensed outlets would be preferable to the tied house system'.[3]

In fairness to the Monopolies Commission, it must be said that they investigated the industry at the time when the period of rapid concentration was coming to an end but the post-merger rationalisation programmes had hardly begun. In other words most of the efficiency gains from the merger movement still lay in the future. Neither could the Commission have foreseen the extent to which the free trade would grow in the years following its report. Nevertheless, the report of the Price Commission suggests that the traditional suspicion of the tied house system has been relatively unaffected by recent changes in the structure and conduct of the industry. It is therefore necessary to analyse these changes in the context of the criticisms made by the

Monopolies Commission, and badly re-iterated by the Price Commission, in order to arrive at a more balanced view of the contemporary nature of competition in the industry.

The Extent and Nature of Competition

The Monopolies Commission argued that the brewers competed with each other in four different ways, the first of these being 'to augment their shares of the market through acquisition of licensed houses'. It was mainained that competition in this field was '. . . most acute among the larger brewers, the tied houses owned by the smaller brewers being their principal potential sources of additional captive outlets for themselves'.[4] Clearly the statement is valid for the fifty-year period ending in 1968, although of course the force of competition through acquisition was for most of the time greatly restrained both by the traditional ethics of gentlemanly behaviour and by the omnipresent reality of family and personal connexions. Since 1968, however, the flow of acquisitions has practically ceased. By the end of the 1960s the national groups had more or less completed their programme of acquisitions and the small number of subsequent purchases have essentially been 'tidying up' operations. The conspicuous exceptions were the entry into the industry firstly of Grand Metropolitan Hotels Ltd. in 1971 (through the acquisition of Truman and Watney Mann) and secondly of Imperial Tobacco Co. Ltd. (through the acquisition of Courage Barclay Simonds). Moreover, since 1972 several of the remaining independent firms have been able to achieve above-average rates of growth. The fear of being left out in the cold has thus been dispelled by the experience of an expanding market and, in particular, by the revival of demand for 'traditional' draught beer. Indeed, the national groups have long accepted that even if they wanted to acquire any of the remaining independents, the cost of doing so would be excessive in relation to the additional trade they would gain. In any case, since the late 1960s all the national groups (and most of the larger independents) have directed much of their effort towards increasing their respective shares of the expanding free trade.

The national brewers have, in fact, reduced their holding of both on- and off-licensed premises in recent years (Tables 4.2 and 4.3).

It is evident from these tables that in the period 1970-74, the number of on- and off-licensed premises owned by brewers declined from 48.5 per cent of the total to 40.4 per cent, against an overall growth of 5.8 per cent in the total number of licensed outlets. Similarly, the tied trade's share of total turnover declined from 55.2 per cent to

Table 4.2 Brewer ownership of on-licensed premises
(including clubs and hotels), 1970-74

Brewers	Numbers				Turnover (£ million)			
	1970	%	1974	%	1970	%	1974	%
Bass								
Charrington	9,736	9.0	9,256	8.2	178.9	10.4	321.4	9.9
Allied	8,265	7.6	7,665	6.8	161.4	9.3	273.6	8.5
Whitbread	9,421	8.7	7,865	6.9	159,7	9.2	242.9	7.5
Watney Mann	6,574	6.0	5,946	5.2	123.5	7.1	219.3	6.8
Courage	6,568	6.0	5,921	5.2	126.5	7.3	220.7	6.8
Scottish &								
Newcastle	1,625	1.5	1,678	1.5	40.4	2.3	83.7	2.6
Other brewers	15,899	14.7	13.800	12.2	271.9	15.7	406.6	12.6
Total brewers	58,088	53.5	52,131	46.0	1,062.3	61.3	1,768.3	54.8
Free trade	50,477	46.5	61.498	54.0	669.1	38.7	1,448.7	45.2
Overall total	108,535		113,629		1,731.4		3,217.0	

Source: *E. I. U. Retail Business*, various issues.

Table 4.3 Brewer ownership of off-licences, 1970-74

Brewers	Numbers				Turnover (£ million)			
	1970	%	1974	%	1970	%	1974	%
Bass								
Charrington	1,640	4.6	990	3.0	16.8	4.1	20.0	2.4
Allied	1,672	5.7	1,300	4.0	29.3	7.2	51.4	6.3
Whitbread	1,284	4.3	865	2.7	18.0	4.4	36.0	4.3
Watney Mann	1,310	4.4	1.110	3.5	19.1	4.7	59.5	7.2
Courage	655	2.2	631	1.9	9.3	2.3	23.0	2.8
Scottish &								
Newcastle	47	0.2	39	0.1	0.9	0.2	1.4	0.1
Other brewers	2,234	7.6	1,860	5.8	26.5	6.5	49.1	6.0
Total brewers	8,842	29.0	6,795	21.0	119.9	29.4	240.4	29.1
Specialist								
multiples	3,340	11.3	3,750	11.6	107.3	26.4	209.0	25.3
Grocery								
multiples	4,619	15.8	5,739	17.8	73.2	18.0	189.2	22.9
Other off-								
licences	12,582	43.9	15,987	49.6	106.2	26.2	187.4	22.7
Total	29,383		32,271		406.6		826.0	

Source: *E. I. U. Retail Business*, various issues.

49.7 per cent, in a period when total turnover nearly doubled. Although comprehensive statistics are not yet available, it is believed that the relative importance of brewer-owned outlets has continued to decline since 1974. Thus, as a form of competition, the acquisition of tied out-lets by brewers in order to increase their market share is no longer of practical significance. The Commission asserted that 'a brewer's best method of increasing his share of the market is to increase his share of the available outlets, since he knows that the ability of other suppliers to compete with him by creating new outlets for their products is severely restricted'.[5] While historically valid, this view was becoming inappropriate even when the Commission expressed it, and continued to lose its relevance during the 1970s as the number of free trade out-lets increased.

It should be added that while the growth of the national groups was based on the acquisition of smaller firms and their houses, the net result was to bring these groups into direct competition with each other. As each group achieved national coverage, so in any given area it had to face competition from at least one and possibly more national groups and additionally from any surviving independent companies. Competi-tion centred not only on the provision of better amenities in public houses but, increasingly, on the supply of well-known brands of keg beer, lager, wines, spirits and soft drinks to the free trade. No national brewer enjoyed anything approaching a regional monopoly and local monopolies were virtually confined to Bristol (Courage) and Norwich (Watney Mann). As the Monopolies Commission pointed out:

> In the past, local monopolies, so far as they existed, were inte-grated monopolies in the sense that a single brewer produced all the beer and owned all the retail outlets in a given area. Such monopolies were protected not only by the tied house system but also by the impracticability of 'importing' draught beer from out-side the area. The new techniques of brewing and distribution have removed this latter protection but have also led to much larger and more widespread chains of tied houses. There is clearly some danger that in some areas particular large brewers may ob-tain dominant positions in the retail trade by absorbing the tied houses of all or most of the brewers in that area. On the other hand, however, these large brewers, in competing with each other to acquire captive outlets, are not inhibited by those considera-tions which would formerly have prevented any brewer from delivering beer outside an area close to his own brewery; and the chains they have formed do . . . overlap to a very considerable extent'.[6]

In short, the development of keg and 'pressurised' beer, by removing

the traditional constraints on the transportation of draught beer in large quantities over long distances, facilitated the emergence of a few large brewery groups based primarily on a nation-wide network of tied houses and increasingly supplemented by an expanding free trade. These groups directly competed with each other in many areas, as even the Monopolies Commission admitted: 'while brewer ownership of public houses is geographically patchy and particular brewers' inn signs are seen more frequently in some areas, in nearly all urban areas there are public houses owned by several different brewers within walking distance of one another'.[7]

The second form of competition between brewers, according to the Commission, was 'to attract custom to their own licensed houses mainly by offering (directly in managed houses or indirectly in tenanted houses) better amenities, service and environment than in the houses of other brewers'. The Commission thought that all brewers competed in this field but pointed out that most of the larger firms tended to concentrate on promoting the group identity of their houses more than on promoting their brands. In fact the tendency to emphasise the corporate 'image' of tied houses became particularly marked during the 1950s among several regional and local firms (for example, Mitchells and Butlers, Tetley, Ind Coope and Massey) who spent relatively large sums in improving their outlets. They did so in response to an unmistakeable trend in consumer demand. The 'improved public house' of the inter-war period had obviously had some effect on popular attitudes towards drinking outside the home. For example, a Hulton Research Survey of 1948 found that of those men who had a favourite public house, only 15 per cent chose it for the quality of its beer; the remainder emphasised its atmosphere, comfort, company, amenities, service and the character of the licensee. As Seldon pointed out in 1955:

> No one in Britain wants people to drink immoderately, least of all the brewers. Therefore, if beer consumption as a whole is to be maintained and increased, it must be done not so much by getting those who drink already to drink more but by getting those who don't drink at all, or very rarely, to make it a habit; regular but moderate. If these people are to accept beer as a regular wholesome drink, it must be done mainly by getting them to accept the public house as a place of general refreshment and relaxation, not only for men but also for women, and not only for the working classes but for all classes. And this they are more likely to do if there is a persistent widening in its services, attractions and amenities.[8]

The growth of real incomes during the late 1950s and 1960s, however, provided a major stimulus to the provision of an even wider range of leisure facilities outside the home and by the same token encouraged competition in the provision of these facilities. As the N.B.P.I. observed in its second report on beer prices (1969):

> Until comparatively recently the pub was regarded as the social centre for those working men whose main relaxation was drinking beer in congenial company. With the coming of a more affluent society the traditional pub has had to face competition from the new entertainment industry — clubs with music and floor shows, discotheques and similar places offering food and entertainment. This external competition requires of the brewers that they do more than maintain existing houses to a traditional standard . . . Increasingly [the brewers] are providing amenities to suit the locality, and the appropriate 'mix' of beers, wines, spirits, soft drinks, food, music, games and so on to meet consumer preferences. In practical terms this involves capital expenditure, both by brewer and licensee, not only on the maintenance of existing amenities but also on the provision of new amenities.[9]

In 1966-69, five large and two smaller breweries surveyed by the N.B.P.I. spent a total of £96 million in improving their tied estate and building new houses. In 1974-77 the same five large breweries spent £227 million in property improvement.[10] In short, the development of a more varied pattern of leisure spending during the 1960s not only intensified the competition between brewers to provide better amenities in their public houses, but also brought the brewers as a whole into competition with suppliers of alternative leisure pursuits.

This tendency for competition to develop between public houses, other catering establishments and other leisure attractions was clearly underlined by the entry into the brewing industry of both Grand Metropolitan Hotels Ltd. and Imperial Tobacco Ltd., and by the (unsuccessful) bid by Allied Breweries for the large hotel group Trust House Forte Ltd. Grand Metropolitan had moved into the catering market through its acquisition of Express Dairies Ltd. (1969) and Berni Inns Ltd. (1970) and had developed its interests in the wider leisure market through Mecca Ltd. (1970). The company's bid for Truman (1971) was thus a logical extension of these interests in so far as the latter owned some 1,250 licensed outlets in London and the South East, many of which had considerable scope for further development.[11] Having acquired Truman, Grand Metropolitan's management began to appreciate the logic of 'going national' in order to exploit fully the production and marketing potential of its diverse interests. The result was a hard-fought but successful bid for Watney Mann.[12] Imperial Tobacco moved into brewing from a large and recently-acquired base in the food industry, underlining yet again the difficulty of maintaining the old demarcation lines around the licensed trade.[13] By the end of the 1960s the concept of public houses as merely outlets for beer was anachronistic. Once it was generally recognised that the public house was only one element within a wider and increasingly sophisticated leisure market, the brewers were faced with the choice of either broadening their traditional role to meet these new requirements or leaving themselves vulnerable to the ambitions of conglomerate firms on the fringes of the brewing industry.

How successful have the brewers been in competing within the leisure market? One rough and ready yardstick is that they have succeeded in reversing the long, secular decline in the consumption of alcoholic drink. By contrast with all other periods of real income growth since the late 1870s, the consumption of all forms of alcoholic drink increased during the 1960s and 1970s. Indeed, an O.P.C.S. survey for the Erroll Committee (1972) found that the greater the income of a household, the higher the proportion spent on drink. The survey also found that as a social habit regular beer drinking had broken out of its traditional occupational confines and had firmly established itself among professional groups.[14] The increasing popularity of alcohol in general is further illustrated by trends in consumer spending (Table 4.4).

Table 4.4 Consumers' expenditure: indices at constant prices

	1961	1966	1971	1973	1975
Food	100	105	109	109	109
Alcoholic drink	100	115	147	179	185
Tobacco	100	98	93	104	98
Housing	100	115	133	140	142
Fuel and light	100	119	127	135	137
Clothing/footwear	100	112	130	145	146
Motor vehicles — purchase	100	162	258	299	214
Motor vehicles — running costs	100	175	231	267	264
Furniture/carpets	100	113	122	136	121
Radio, electrical and other durables	100	117	166	248	226
Books, magazines, etc.	100	100	93	99	91
Chemists' goods	100	119	139	180	190
Communications	100	122	156	201	241
Travel	100	103	107	121	114
Entertainment/recreation	100	122	139	169	184
Total expenditure	100	114	126	140	138

Source: Social Trends, 1975, C.S.O., p. 132.

These figures suggest that consumer spending on alcohol has kept pace with that on entertainment and recreation in general. Moreover, the share of alcohol in total consumer spending increased from 6.1 per cent in 1960-64 to 8.3 per cent in 1972-76.[15] Further confirmation of this trend may be gained from comparing the results of two surveys of popular drinking habits. A Hulton survey of 1952 found that only 30 per cent of men drank beer regularly (i.e. more than once a week); the O.P C.S. Survey of 1970 suggested that 61 per cent of men were regular beer drinkers. In 1952 only one in seventeen women came into the 'regular' category; in 1970 this had grown to one in four.[16] Thus between 1960 and 1972 the average retail price of alcoholic drink rose by 74 per cent, whereas *per capita* expenditure on alcohol increased by 187 per cent. If the two surveys quoted above are reliable, this trend would seem to indicate that more non-drinkers were becoming occasional drinkers, and that more of the latter were moving into the 'regular' category.

It may, of course, be argued that a considerable proportion of this growth is attributable to the expansion of the take-home trade, which would have occurred regardless of any revival in public house consumption. While this is undoubtedly true, it would also appear that the brewers' investment in their licensed estates has borne fruit. In sharp contrast to the 1920s, the younger generation of the 1960s began to visit public houses in large numbers and on a regular basis. Thus the O.P.C.S. Survey quoted above found that in the 18-24 age group, 75 per cent said that they visited a public house at least once a month (compared with only 18 per cent in the over-65 age group). More generally, it was discovered that nearly three quarters of the adult population visited a public house at least occasionally and 44 per cent were 'regulars' (i.e. once a month or more often). This is perhaps hardly surprising in view of the fact that nearly two thirds of the adults in the survey felt that public houses were 'warm, friendly places', in which social intercourse assumed a much more important role than the availability of drink. The provision of food in snack form and of proper toilet and washing facilities were also thought to be important by a majority of those in the survey. This does not, of course, mean that most people are now wholly satisfied with the amenities offered in public houses. Indeed, the survey quoted above revealed a widespread demand for extended family facilities within public houses, a demand which has always been extremely difficult to meet due to the determination of Parliament and licensing justices to discourage children from visiting public houses. Nevertheless, the social status of the public house has undoubtedly been greatly improved since the 1950s, and the active interest of the brewers in this field must obviously be regarded as the principal agent of change. As Gooding has argued:

> They spent heavily on the pubs, making them attractive to women and therefore doubled the potential numbers of customers. Young people deserted the coffee bars for the pubs too, once the pub had shrugged off the old 'image' that branded it a place that only the middle-aged and older people would find amenable. The survival of the pub as a 'leisure centre' in the face of the onslaught of the television age — an onslaught that has significantly damaged other leisure businesses like the cinema and soccer — bears witness to the marketing skills the brewers employed during the hectic years of change.[17]

Another form of competition discussed by the Monopolies Commission arises from the brewers' desire '. . . to penetrate each other's captive markets by developing — through advertising and other forms of sales promotion — brands which become known on a more or less national scale, so that consumers tend to demand them at licensed houses not owned by their producers'.[18] The Commission maintained that these efforts were particularly directed towards the houses of the smaller brewers which each national group could penetrate without necessarily conceding equivalent penetration of another group's brands in its own houses. It was in fact conceded that the very existence of reciprocal trade tended to show that the tied house system had not restricted competition between different brands to the extent that it might have done. To the extent that a brewer supplied 'foreign' beers to his tied houses he widened the range of brands available to his customers, even though he imposed a surcharge of 5-15 per cent on the wholesale price to his tenants. The Commission obviously thought that the practice of surcharging 'foreign' beers was designed to discourage customers from buying them, especially if 'foreign' brands directly competed with brands supplied by the brewer himself. The success of discriminatory pricing was inferred from the fact that while practically every brewer sold some beer supplied by another brewer, the share of 'foreign' beer amounted to little more than 10 per cent of total beer sales through tied houses, and half of this was accounted for by Guinness's stout and the remainder by a small number of national brands.[19] In reality, however, the significance of reciprocal trading was tending to decline during the 1960s. Vaizey, for example, calculated that in the early 1950s, approximately 15 per cent of beer sold through tied outlets was composed of national brands supplied under reciprocal arrangements.[20] During the 1950s the 'foreign' trade was of considerable importance to firms such as Ind Coope and Whitbread for the simple reason that it provided the only way of achieving anything approaching national coverage through the tied trade. With the emergence of competing national chains of tied houses during the 1960s, however, and the simultaneous expansion of the free trade, reciprocal trading gradually assumed a secondary role in the marketing strategy of most of the national brewers. With the decline of bottled beer and the corresponding growth of keg beers and lager, the national brewers concentrated on pushing these brands in the free trade and only to a lesser extent in the small independent brewery sector.[21]

The free trade was in fact the fourth and final area of competition between brewers to which the Commission drew attention. The nature of competition in the free trade was of particular interest to the Commission in so far as it involved both the quality of the product and the price at which it was supplied. The growth of the free trade has been described earlier in this chapter and no repetition is needed here. It must be emphasised, however, that success in the free trade as a whole depends not simply on price competitiveness but on the possession of a national distribution network and heavily-advertised national brands. Not surprisingly, the Price Commission found that the small and regional brewers were considerably more dependent on their own tied trade than the large brewers, who between them sold almost as much beer to the free trade as to their own licensed houses.[22] Two additional points should be made. Firstly, although both wholesale and retail price competition has long been an important feature of the free trade, the brewers (in common with bulk suppliers in any industry) tend to discriminate between free outlets according to their turnover, with the biggest customers receiving the biggest wholesale price discounts. Secondly, the acuteness of price competition has not prevented the growth of the loan-tie as a method of securing trade, particularly in the club sector. Although there are no up-to-date estimates of the relative significance of brewery loans in the club trade, it is believed that the national brewers and some of the larger independents have been increasing their loan business since the late 1960s.[23] But to the extent that the loan-tie is a significant factor in the free trade, it suggests that even in an expanding market the natural response of most suppliers to strong competition is to seek a measure of security by exploiting the various advantages which large-scale operation has given them *vis-à-vis* the independent retailer.

The Tied Public House System and Competition
The main thrust of the Commission's attack on the tied house system

was the discouraging effect which it allegedly had on price competition in the retail trade:

> . . . competition between the public houses of different brewers appears to us to take the form largely of rivalry in amenities. We recognise that this has contributed to improved standards of amenities in public houses. But competition is concentrated upon amenities because price competition is largely absent and because the brewers' attitude to retailing affects the attitude of the tenants.[24]

The Commission considered that as a result of the brewers' direct involvement in the on-licensed trade through their ownership of public houses, the normal oligopolistic reluctance to engage in price competition had been transmitted from the supply side of the industry to the retailing side:

> Price competition between tied houses would mean price competition between brewers. The brewers in general would have to stand the adverse effects of retail price competition on the level of their prices and profits, without compensating benefits. We do not think that brewers, especially having regard to their investments in tied houses for the sake of market security wish to compete with each other in this way, which would be largely self-defeating from each brewer's point of view.[25]

To substantiate its proposition that a greater degree of retail price competition would have occurred had the tied house system not existed, the Commission quoted the acuteness of price competition in the free off-licensed trade. The comparison drawn with the free off-licensed trade, however, is invalid. The character of competitive relationships in the on-licensed trade is and always has been determined by the nature of beer retailing itself and not by the presence or absence of vertical integration. In the 'take-home' trade, the emphasis is clearly on the sale of the product as such and consumers — as with other proprietary goods — tend to be influenced by price differentials between competing outlets, hence the rapid growth of liquor retailing in supermarkets. The same can hardly be said, however, of 'on-sale' custom, where the beer consumed is part of a wider package of amenities and its price is thus only one of the factors which influence customer decisions. As the Brewers' Society argued in its evidence to the Commission:

> Choice [of brands] is only one element in the package which the pub offers. The rest of the package consists of the standard of furnishings and decorations; facilities for games; availability of food; the personalities of the licensees; and the company to be found in the house. Thus . . . the price of a pint is compounded of two elements, the product itself and the provision of the environment in which its consumption is enjoyed.[26]

If the price of beer were all-important in the on-licensed trade, it would be impossible for brewers and licensees to maintain the customary price differential between their public and saloon bars. It would also be difficult to explain the ability of most free houses to compete for the retail trade against tied houses, since prices in the former tend, on average, to be significantly higher than in the latter.[27] Again, if price competition were decisive, the growth of clubs (where prices have always tended to be lower than in neighbouring public houses because clubs are usually non-profit making organisations) would surely have been much more rapid than it has been. In fact, however, the Commission claimed that clubs and public houses were not on the whole 'in direct competition' because they catered for different needs, offering different 'packages' of amenities.[28] Interestingly this conclusion was in direct contrast to that reached by the Royal Commission of 1929-31, which believed that many licensed clubs fulfilled 'substantially the same purpose as a public house'. The fairest conclusion would probably be that clubs do compete for much the same business as public houses, but that this competition is much stronger in some areas of the country (e.g. South Wales, the North East, Lancashire) than in others.

A further claim advanced by the Monopolies Commission was that the unwillingness of brewers to encourage price competition in the tied trade was reflected in the business attitudes of tenant licensees:

> The tenants who are appointed are those who, in general, are prepared to work under the restraints insisted upon by their brewer landlords. They therefore tend to be of a somewhat homogeneous type, modest in their commercial ambitions and not aggressively competitive in their business attitudes. The effect is to blunt such incentives to competition among public houses as might otherwise exist within the confines of restrictive licensing.

The Commission regarded the 'wet rent' system as symptomatic of the lack of incentives to compete:

> The fact that rent varies with turnover may not positively discourage a really enterprising tenant from seeking to expand his sales at the expense of other public houses; but the 'wet rent' system — as opposed to a system of fixed rentals only — is inhibiting in that it reduces for the tenant the additional profit to be gained from additional competitive effort and enterprise. Thus if the tenant is of limited ambition he might prefer — by keeping his bar prices up — to earn his living on the basis of a modest turnover with consequent modest rent.[29]

Here the Commission was on firmer ground. It was indicated above that the 'wet rent' system was designed to help tenants make a reasonable living in an era when beer consumption was tending to fall and the number of licensed houses was excessive in relation to the total volume of trade. The system survived so long partly because the decline in beer consumption continued for so long and partly because it had become part of the framework of custom and practice within the industry.

By the late 1960s, however, the over-supply of licensed outlets had long ceased to be a problem, and the upward trend in consumer demand opened up new possibilities for entrepreneurship in the retail trade. The defensive orientation of the 'wet rent' system was no longer appropriate to the market environment. It was also becoming increasingly clear that both brewers and tenants were less satisfied with the traditional approach to rents than they had once been. The National Federation of Licensed Victuallers argued before both the Monopolies Commission and the N.B.P.I that the high wholesale prices charged to the tied trade by the brewers were becoming increasingly incompatible with the brewers' traditional insistence on fixing maximum retail prices for the public bars of their tied houses. Tenants' retail margins were being subject to a double squeeze and yet at the same time they were given little incentive to increase their income. Thus the Federation called for the abolition of public bar price control and for the introduction of a system of 'sole' rents. The brewers for their part were becoming increasingly dissatisfied with the low return on their tied property, partly because during the 1960s they had invested heavily in improving their houses. One solution was, of course, to transfer selected houses from tenancy to direct management, and most of the major groups adopted this policy to a greater or less degree.[30] Nevertheless, given the overwhelming preponderance of tenanted houses throughout the industry, this was not a comprehensive solution. As the chairman of Watney Mann observed at his company's annual meeting in 1971:

> I am firmly convinced that tenanted houses will continue to represent the major part of our licensed estate. New conditions must be created, however, to enable the tenant to take the maximum advantage of trading opportunities and for the company to achieve a satisfactory return on its investment in this sector.

The chairman of Bass Charrington was more explicit: 'We believe that there is an continued future for the efficient and forward-looking licensee and special training facilities exist to make improvement possible. But tenanted houses must make their contribution to the company's profitability and they must be rented on realistic terms'.[31] As a result, in the period 1970-72 most of the major groups negotiated new 'charters' with their tenants which, among other things, abolished 'wet rent', increased the level of property rents, freed tenants from public bar price control and gave them improved security of tenure. Henceforward most tenants were supplied with their beers, wines and spirits at free trade prices and were given more discretion in their pricing policies, in return for which the brewers began to raise property rents to more realistic levels. This radical change in brewer-tenant relations has not, however, led to aggressive price competition in the tied trade for the simple reason that the price of beer remains of limited significance in relation to other elements within the total 'package' on offer in public houses.

From a public policy perspective, therefore, it is questionable whether price competition has any real operational significance when applied to the on-licensed trade. Indeed, it may be argued that no one can objectively assess the value of all the different amenities provided in the 'package' since each individual customer is likely to have his own view of what constitutes an optimal mix. The 'package' concept does, however, encourage price flexibility, and this has recently attracted the attention of the Price Commission. In a survey of bar prices by type of house, the Commission found that while price differences between managed and tied tenanted houses were 'very small', there were some 'striking' variations in the price of certain types of beer (especially lager) and that average prices in free houses were 'invariably higher' than in brewery-owned outlets. The Commission's survey of gross percentage margins by type of house, however, revealed much wider variations on different beers, but with free houses again enjoying consistently higher margins.[32] The apparent absence of an 'exact relationship between prices and costs' led the Commission to conclude that the brewers' pricing policy (especially on lager) has been geared to what they believe 'the market will stand' and that their managed houses have led prices upward. Yet this analysis begs more questions than it answers. If managed houses are the price leaders, why do free houses charge higher prices and receive higher gross margins than either managed or tenanted houses? The Commission lamely admitted that it had 'not been possible to explore fully' the reasons for the significant price differentials between free and tied houses.[33] If the retail margins on the same kind of beers in the same kind of houses are not absolutely identical does this necessarily imply a lack of competition between them? If, by contrast, margins *were* identical, would this not imply the possibility of collusion between brewers and licensees? By the same token, why should there be an 'exact' relationship between wholesale prices and costs? The cost structure of every company is different, reflecting to some extent differences in efficiency, and their wholesale price strategies will no doubt reflect, at least to some degree, the current level of demand for their beers and the strength of the competition. The growing importance of the free trade, and the role of retail and wholesale price competition in that sector, must in any case tend to narrow the gap between costs and prices. It may not be coincidental, therefore, that in 1974-76 the net wholesale profit margins of the large brewers, who are all heavily committed to the free trade, were markedly narrower than those of either the regional or the small brewers.[34] It would be reasonable to conclude, therefore, that while the advent of 'cut-price' liquor retailing has undoubtedly encouraged both competition and expansion in one sector of the market, it would be unrealistic to expect that it must or should have a similar effect in the on-licensed trade. The emphasis on competition through amenities in the on-licensed trade derives essentially from the character of the retailing operation itself and not from the presence of vertical integration. To condemn the tied house system simply because it has 'not brought lower prices' is, therefore, to misunderstand its fundamental nature.[35]

The Tied House System and Barriers to Entry

The Commission was also concerned about the role of the tied house system in preventing the entry of new producers and new products into the industry. Proponents of the concept of 'workable competition' have long thought it desirable that new enterprises should be able to enter an industry because of the salutary effects that new competitors may have on the market conduct of established companies. In reality, however, unfettered entry by new enterprises is rarely encountered. In most industries barriers to entry exist which the newcomer must first negotiate before he can establish himself in the market. These barriers may be structural, institutional or financial in character. In structural terms, it must be recognised firstly that established companies with substantial market shares and large-scale production and distribution facilities may have a decisive cost advantage; secondly that strong consumer preferences may well favour the established companies; and thirdly that market outlets and/or essential raw material supplies may have been pre-empted. In institutional terms, established firms may have the advantage of owning patents, franchises, licences and exclusive dealing contracts. In financial terms, the new entrant may have to make a massive investment in large-scale production plant, advertising and product development, which he is unlikely to do unless the industry itself is profitable and expanding.

Although the mere threat of entry may be sufficient to influence the competitive behaviour of established firms, actual entry can be expected to have a more decisive impact. The term 'new entrant' itself frequently causes confusion. Actual entry may be effected either by a newcomer establishing new manufacturing capacity ('classic' entry) or by the acquisition or transferance of the assets of an existing producer ('take-over' entry). In the literature on industrial organisation, the term 'new entry' is usually used to describe the 'classic' method — i.e. the appearance of an additional supplier in the market under independent ownership. It is generally assumed that 'classic' entry will, by enlarging the number of independent suppliers of the product concerned, intensify competitive pressures in the industry, although this does not always follow. It would, however, be a mistake to assume that 'take-over' entry seldom has more than a neutral effect on competition. Admittedly, the number of competitors is left unchanged and the diversified entrant may be quickly assimilated into the established *modus operandi* of the industry without disturbing the existing relationship between the other firms. But it may also be the case that aggressive diversification by outsiders who have a wider perception of the industry's capabilities than the established firms, may do much to alter both the accepted ways of doing business and the structure of the industry itself.

While most of the impediments to entry listed above exist to some extent in the brewing industry, the combination of restrictive licensing and the tied house system has frequently been singled out by official investigators as the primary reason for the paucity of new entrants. It is argued that the pre-emption of existing retail outlets by established companies, together with the limited availability of new outlets, have denied access to potential entrants. The claim was first heard in 1817 when the Parliamentary committee on 'Public Breweries' in London pointed out that a policy which restricted the number of licensed houses but did not attempt to prevent the brewers from controlling more of these houses, inevitably restricted entry into the industry by small entrepreneurs. Yet the real barrier to entry into the London trade was not the tied house system as such but the fact that the brewers of central London were already exploiting the economies of large-scale production. Up to the 1870s neither a permissive licensing system nor an expanding market were sufficient to over-ride the capital costs of direct entry into the London trade. Only the major Burton brewers (who, significantly, were also achieving the economies of large-scale production from 1840 onwards) were able to challenge the big London firms in their own market. It should also be remembered that between 1820 and 1890 it was customary in London to tie outlets by loan, not by ownership of the lease. As such the tie was vulnerable to competition and in itself posed no barrier to new entrants. In the provinces, tied trade was a reality long before restrictive licensing made it essential, but entry into the industry for the small entrepreneur remained relatively easy up to the 1970s. New entrants were encouraged firstly by the expanding market for beer and the consequent opportunities for profit, and secondly by the low capital cost of establishing 'economic' production plant. When these two inducements disappeared — as they did during the 1870s — the flow of new entrants dried up. Restrictive licensing and the tied house system certainly added to the costs of entry, but even if they had not existed it is difficult to see how the industry would have continued to attract a significant number of new entrants in the conditions which prevailed after 1880.

Nevertheless, subsequent investigators have continued to insist that the tied house system is *the* obstacle to new entry. As the N.B.P.I. contended in its first report on beer prices (1966): 'This formidable barrier to new entrants has ensured that the methods of doing business — manufacturing, wholesaling and retailing — are set almost exclusively by those who were in the trade at the start of this century'.[36] The same point was re-iterated, with even less justification, by the Price Commission. Yet while it cannot be denied that the tied house system is *one* impediment to entry, the industry is by no means as 'closed' as the statement quoted above suggests. It has been pointed out earlier in this chapter that the 'captive' trade of the brewers has been in relative decline for many years. The introduction of a more liberal approach to the issue of new licences, especially off-licences, in 1961 has helped to encourage a rapid expansion in the number of free outlets, so that by 1976 brewery-owned outlets amounted to only 36 per cent of the total.[37] It can no longer be said, therefore, that market access conditions in the industry entirely preclude the possibility of 'classic' entry, although the newcomer would, of course, still have to contend with the barriers raised by economies of scale and product differentiation. Yet even in markets where established suppliers have pre-empted existing outlets, where new outlets are unobtainable, and where economies of scale and product differentiation barriers are substantial, opportunities for 'take-over' entry may still exist. The main reason why 'take-over' entry is relatively new to the brewing industry is not the extent of the tied house system but the fact that up to the late 1950s demand for beer seemed to be locked into a long-term secular decline. The industry did not in fact become an attractive proposition to the growth-oriented conglomerate companies until the consumption of its main product began to increase, its structure became much more concentrated, and it began to improve the return on its assets. A particularly important development, as noted above, was the emergence of an increasingly sophisticated leisure market in which several different industries and services were seen to be in direct competition. When all these factors came together — as they did in the early 1970s — the traditional assumption that new entrants could be kept out of the industry either by the tied house system *per se* or by collusive action on the part of the brewery 'establishment' was rapidly disproved. It is therefore quite wrong to argue, as the Price Commission did, that by blocking new entrants the tied house system has ensured that '. . . there has been little change over the years in the way business, whether wholesale or retail, is done'.[38] The extent to which the conduct of business has changed becomes fully apparent when one examines the retail trade itself.

Finally, the contention that the tied house system has hindered the entry of new products should be treated with scepticism. It must be conceded that in a market where there are specialised tastes for beers and that market is adequately supplied by well-established brewers, it is likely to be difficult for new entrants to establish themselves in precisely the same field. The historical experience of Guinness and to a lesser extent Bass, however, suggests that product differentiation and superior quality may enable firms to achieve and maintain a national demand for their products which does not depend on the ownership of retail outlets. The growth of lager sales during the 1960s also underlines the flexibility of the system. Initially most lager was imported from abroad (86 per cent in 1960) and was sold by British brewers through their tied houses. As the popularity of lager grew, so more indigenous firms began to brew their own, even though this required new plant, and by 1976 only 7 per cent of lager consumption was imported.[39] The rapid growth of domestic lager production, therefore, reinforces the conclusion that the tied house system has not hindered the entry of new products irrespective of consumer demand. Indeed, it could be argued that the national brewers are, because of their distribution systems, in a particularly strong position to develop and market new products. It should certainly be borne in mind that bottled beer, keg beer and draught lager were all in their turn taken up and extensively promoted by the national brewers.

5 Performance and Efficiency

Production and Distribution Efficiency

It was noted earlier that one major criticism which the Monopolies Commission made of the tied house system was that it had retarded the elimination of inefficient and redundant production capacity:

> The ownership of tied houses has in itself afforded the less efficient brewers some protection . . . concentration of brewing capacity and the elimination of the less efficient brewers, have not proceeded as far or as fast as they would have done if a large part of the industry had not already been vertically integrated. Elimination of less efficient units has depended too much on the ability of the more efficient and aggressive brewers to acquire sufficient protected shares of the market through mergers involving large-scale investments on their part, including the acquisition of some assets not required for their own sake.[1]

Once again, however, the Commission was basing its view on what it believed had happened in the past. It has already been indicated that during the inter-war period both the pace of concentration and the efficiency gains from post-merger rationalisation were restricted by the prevailing framework of family control and the brewers' sense of social responsibility. This does not, of course, imply that the tied house system played no part in keeping small firms in existence. Obviously it did. As late as 1948, for example, some 174 breweries produced less than 45,000 barrels a year, despite the general belief in the industry that an output of 50-60,000 barrels was the threshold of 'economic' production. Vaizey concluded: 'The tied house system has the effect of maintaining many small breweries in operation in markets which the transport costs of bringing beer from a distance would not protect . . . a large number of existing breweries, possibly 250 or more, are kept in existence because of a monopolistic practice'.[2] The staple product of most small breweries at this time (as in previous decades) was cheap draught beer which, because of its perishability, had to be sold within a relatively short distance. As long as this beer could be sold locally at a profit, then it was economic to go on producing it.

But, as the Commission itself conceded, the tied house system has never been so rigid as to exclude all other brewers' products from the outlets of a particular company. Some degree of competitive pressure has always been present, and thus the tied house system has not provided small firms with an impregnable defence against changes in consumer demand. During the 1950s the market strength of cheap, local draught beer was being eroded by the continued growth of national and regional bottled beer. In the following decade tastes swung in favour of national keg beers and lagers. In this situation many small brewers found themselves at a disadvantage *vis-à-vis* their regional and national competitors. Nor could they resist the demand for better and more varied amenities in public houses. Thus in the course of the 1950s many small to middle-sized firms came to recognise that their resources were insufficient to meet the combined demands of property improvement and product development. It is hardly surprising, therefore, that their directors decided to sell out to an acceptable competitor as soon as a favourable opportunity presented itself.

In any industry where substantial economies of scale exist, there is a strong tendency for output to become concentrated in large plants. The main areas within the brewing process in which economies can be made by increasing production capacity are indicated in Tables 5.1 and 5.2.

Table 5.1 *Structure of brewing costs 1965*

	Production, excise duty and distribution costs* (% of total)	Typical production costs per barrel for breweries with a capacity of 0.5m barrels	
		Existing brewery	New brewery
Brewery materials	8.6	2.40	2.40
Direct labour	7.2	1.53	0.33
Depreciation	2.8	0.45	1.43
Other costs (purchasing, cleaning materials, power etc.)	12.9	1.86	1.86
Total production costs	31.5	6.24	6.02
Excise duty	61.4	—	—
Distribution costs	7.1	—	—

Source: C. F. Pratten, *Economies of Scale in Manufacturing Industry*, Cambridge University Press, 1971, p. 74.

*Based on National Board for Prices and Incomes (1966 Report) Data — average costs for 40 breweries.

Table 5.2   Economies of scale for new breweries
(indices of unit costs)

Annual output capacity (m bulk barrels)	Capital	Labour	Value added	Total costs* (average)	(marginal)
0.1	125	191	130	113	—
0.2	100	100	100	100	87
0.5	55	60	56	81	68
1.0	35	48	36	72	63

Source: Pratten, op. cit., p. 75.
*Figures include materials but exclude excise duty and transport costs.

It will be seen that in the mid-1960s, excise duty accounted for well over half, and production costs for one third of total costs. The figures suggest that substantial savings in labour costs can be achieved in new plants, the main reason being that many old plants have been gradually extended over a long period of time and as such are not designed to take full advantage of their scale. The fall in the index of unit labour costs reflects increases in productivity as fewer employees operate larger blocks of capital equipment. The unit costs of raw materials, by contrast, depend primarily on the strength of the beer being produced and are not much affected by plant size.[3] A further point to remember is that capital investment costs are obviously much higher for a new plant, so that the latter must attract a correspondingly higher depreciation charge. In short, the construction of new brewing plant does not bring savings in every stage of the production process, nor can the estimates quoted above allow for possible uneconomic aspects of size such as increased vulnerability to strikes and other stoppages. Nevertheless, since the 1950s the changing pattern of consumer demand and the emergence of the national groups have together brought about a steady reduction in the number of production units and a corresponding increase in the output of the remainder (Table 5.3). Some national groups, however, have advanced much further in this field than others (Table 5.4).

These differences are mainly attributable to two factors — firstly, the size of the rationalisation problem which groups inherited from the past, and secondly the degree of product specialisation achieved by each group. In the case of both Whitbread and Bass, the acquisition of a national chain of tied outlets entailed the acquisition of a relatively large number of small production units. While some of these breweries have been phased out and replaced by very large plants, the commitment

Table 5.3 *The pattern of production, 1940-76*

	Number of breweries	Average output per brewery ('000 barrels)
1940	840	30.0
1950	367	46.0
1960	358	73.4
1968	211	146.0
1973	163	217.0
1976	147	268.0

Source: The Brewers' Society.

of both groups to maintain a strong presence in the regional draught beer market has induced them to retain certain breweries which might, on strictly economic grounds, have been closed.[4] Scottish and Newcastle, by contrast, inherited a relatively small rationalisation problem from its two major constituent parts and since its formation has concentrated on the production of a relatively small range of national brands. Nevertheless, it would appear that since 1970 all the major groups have been planning and building production plant on an unprecedented scale. Although Table 5.2 refers only to breweries of up to one million barrels capacity, data from the American brewing industry suggests that scale economies continue beyond this point.[5] Indeed almost all the major groups have either built or planned production units with capacity in excess of 1.5 million barrels before 1980.[6] Putting the brewing industry in a wider context, Wood has shown that in 1963-74 its record in terms of capital expenditure per head of those employed was well above average. In a group of 22 capital-intensive industries, brewing and malting ranked eighth in terms of expenditure per head, or more than three times the average for all manufacturing industries.[7]

Would the concentration of productive capacity have proceeded more quickly in the absence of the tied houses system, as the Monopolies Commission alleged? In favour of the Commission's argument, it could be said that some small firms might have disappeared earlier than they did had they not enjoyed a considerable degree of market security. On the other hand, it must also be noted that the reduction in the number of breweries summarised in Table 5.3 is broadly comparable with trends abroad. In the USA, for example, the number of breweries fell from 756 in 1945 to 187 in 1966; over the same period there was a reduction from 653 to 144 in France, from 143 to 55 in Sweden and from 83 to 33 in the Netherlands. Brewery ownership of retail outlets is legally prohibited in all these countries. If, therefore, the process of

Table 5.4 Brewing plant rationalisation
by major producers, 1958-76

	Breweries owned in 1958 and subsequent acquisitions	Breweries in operation in 1970	Average plant capacity, 1970 (000 b.bls.)	Breweries in operation in 1976	Average plant capacity, 1976 (000 b.bls.)
Bass Charrington	38	21	305	12	650
Allied	16	9	600	7	954
Whitbread	33	18	228	19	268
Watney/G.M.H.	13	11	282	8	587
Scottish and Newcastle	8	3	933	3	1,446
Courage	14	6	366	8	437
Guinness	1	1	1,700	2	3,500
Others	237	121	66	89	39

Source: *The Brewery Manual*, 1958 and 1970; *E. I. U. Retail Business*, No. 226.

concentration in the UK has been slower than it should have been, other factors besides the tied houses system must be involved. Firstly, if it is assumed that regional and local preferences would still have existed in a free market, it must be accepted that brewers would still have attached considerable importance to meeting these tastes. Indeed, it could be argued that in the absence of captive outlets, brewers would have been even more sensitive to local tastes and preferences than they were since customer goodwill would have been easier to lose. In this situation, the brewers might well have been under considerable pressure to keep uneconomic local breweries in production. Moreover, ever since the First World War, the inclusion of excise duty in total production costs has tended to close the gap between efficient and inefficient plants. In Vaizey's words:

> The duty makes costs more uniform for beer brewed at the same gravity and reduces the scope for retail price competition based upon manufacturing efficiency; but since quality and gravity can be varied, the price per unit of 'quality' is not uniform. Since consumers are not expert judges, there is wide scope for imperfections in the market; as a result the relative prices of different beers are not closely tied to differences in production costs. Possibly, if the duty were lower, the lower costs of the more efficient brewers would enable them to reduce prices and maintain quality. As a force making for concentration, technical economies would be more important in a less taxed and less imperfect market, because the cost differences between brewers would give greater opportunity for price and quality competition. As it is, manufacturing economies add to profits without significantly attracting custom.[8]

In short, the scope for price competition has traditionally been limited by product differentiation and by the importance of excise duty as a proportion of total costs. It is therefore misleading to argue that if the tied house system had not existed, price competition would have been much more prevalent and that inefficient production capacity would thus have been eliminated much more rapidly.

The Commission also argued that the tied house system was 'to some extent detrimental to (as well as being inessential to) the creation by brewers of 'rational' and efficient systems of distribution in contemporary conditions'.[9] How valid was this criticism? It must be said at the outset that a long-standing problem for many brewery companies has been that of balancing the economies of centralised production against the costs of transportation and distribution. The main determinant of unit transport costs is the quantity of beer delivered per vehicle mile, and this is not systematically related to plant size. The level of transport costs incurred by any brewery has always depended very much on the characteristics of its market. In high density urban areas where retail outlets are relatively numerous, unit transport costs are considerably lower than in sparsely populated rural areas. It is worth recalling, by way of illustration, that by the early nineteenth century the London trade had moved decisively in favour of concentrated, large-scale production because it served the biggest urban market in the UK. The economies of large-scale production were not, therefore, offset by higher distribution costs. A few of the Burton brewers subsequently achieved even higher levels of output and still managed to distribute their beer over the national rail network. Even so the major Burton brewers remained heavily dependent on the London market, while their relatively high distribution costs were partly absorbed by the independent wholesalers and bottlers who handled their beer. Most of the smaller provincial brewers, by contrast, were confined within a 15 mile radius of their production plants, particularly as the tied house system developed. The growth of the bottled beer trade between the wars and its development on a national scale during the postwar period once again underlined the significance of transport costs. Weight has always been a major factor in the distribution of beer. For bottled beer, the weight of the bottle itself contributes about 60 per cent of the total load. Consequently, the national and major regional companies found that it was far cheaper to decentralise their bottling stores and feed them by bulk tankers. The same considerations apply to keg beer and lager, a substantial proportion of which is supplied in bulk to a network of depots and is then 'packaged' for distribution to the retail trade.

With the growth of the national brewery groups and the concommitant development of a national market for keg beers and lager, so transport costs became relatively more important. In the late 1960s, the N.B.P.I reported that distribution costs represented 18 per cent of total costs exclusive of excise duty, nearly two thirds of which was accounted for by labour.[10] The search for further economies in distribution has therefore continued and long-range deliveries have been made more cost-efficient. This has been done firstly by the extensive use of articulated vehicle units which make 'shuttle-running' easier to organise – an integrated 'shuttle service' can obtain the maximum use of the total transportation capacity of a vehicle by round-the-clock working. Secondly, the maximum load which a vehicle is permitted to carry has been increased from 15 to 20 tons. Thirdly, computers have been used to analyse demand information, geographical details and cost data and produce the cheapest pattern of deliveries. Finally, the installation of bulk beer tanks in a significant number of retail outlets has effectively by-passed the depot and the 'packaging' stage of the distribution process by facilitating direct delivery from the brewery.

The Commission, while conceding that the brewers had been able to achieve considerable savings in distribution by applying new techniques, still maintained that these savings were not necessarily greater than, or even as great as, those that might have been achieved if the main retail outlets had not been tied to particular brewers through ownership:

> In such circumstances brewers might be delivering to independent wholesalers, independent chains of retailers and individually-owned outlets; and it could well be that, if prices were adjusted to reflect savings from scale and regularity of delivery and the incidence of transport costs, such a system could be more economical than the present one.[11]

This contention was unsupported by empirical evidence. Indeed it is curious that the Commission did not ask the brewers to submit cost calculations involving alternative arrangements, as it did, for example, in its investigation of petrol supply.[12] While the new distribution techniques noted above would almost certainly have been introduced in the absence of the tied house system, the contention that a distribution system based on the free trade would be more economical than the existing one is, to say the least, questionable.

While the general evidence on distribution systems indicates that it is not normally necessary for a supplier to obtain exclusive control of outlets in order to secure low-cost distribution, the tied house system has, because of the peculiar characteristics of beer retailing, almost certainly resulted in lower distribution costs than would otherwise have been achieved. Economies in distribution under the tied house system have arisen firstly because brewers have been able to deliver to a smaller number of retail outlets than would have been the case under independent retailing, and secondly because the average size of the loads delivered has been greater. Historically, the geographical compactness of many brewers' chains of tied houses has been a significant factor in keeping physical distribution costs and associated 'overhead' expenses down to a minimum. A further factor is that with captive outlets, the level of demand can be ascertained more effectively, thereby facilitating the economical loading and routing of vehicles. This has been particularly important in the case of traditional cask beer because of its short life. The fact that a large and growing proportion of the major brewers' deliveries are now made to free trade outlets and involve long-life keg beers and lagers in no way invalidates these observations. The cost of including free trade outlets in a concentrated tied trade operation is small compared with a decentralised, exclusively free trade system of distribution, so that free trade deliveries have been easily integrated into tied trade distribution networks. In this context it is interesting to note the distribution arrangements for Guinness which, it will be recalled, has no public houses. According to the managing director of the company:

> With Guinness the fact that it is delivered in bulk to brewers all over the country and is then bottled by them and distributed in their own trucks to their own houses in full loads — mixed loads with everything that the house wants — keeps distribution costs down to the absolute minimum.[13]

Profits and Investment

Firm and industry profit rates, conventionally measured as a rate of return on capital employed, are of interest in so far as they reflect the efficiency with which the firm or industry uses its resources. If profits are low this may be an indication that the firm is inefficient. On the other hand, high profits may not necessarily reflect superior efficiency but instead may result from a firm being able to exploit its market power. In the case of the brewing industry, taking a long-run perspective, profits have neither been unduly low or 'excessive' when compared with the average return for British industry as a whole. Profit rates, however, need to be looked at in the context of an industry's risk status and investment requirements and it is the case, of course, that industries differ considerably in these respects. As regards the former consideration the brewing industry has for long been viewed as a 'low risk' sector.

The N.B.P.I. summed up the risk status of the industry in its 1966 Report thus:

> By and large, we take the view that brewing is less risky than many other industries. There is indeed some indication of this in the industry's methods of finance. The ratio of loan capital (with a prior claim on profits) to equity capital is high. For the eight main brewing companies, long-term loans are equal to 27 per cent of capital employed (compared with an average for industry as a whole of 12 per cent). The attraction to the lending institutions of lending to brewery companies is the knowledge that, even if the brewing business were to fail, there are considerable realisable properties. From the point of view of the brewery companies themselves, however, their readiness to incur a substantial weight of prior charge obligations would seem to argue a measure of confidence in the stability of profits.[14]

While the industry's risk status may be indeed as low as the N.B.P.I. suggests, its need for enormous sums of investment funds is beyond dispute. The construction of new breweries and the up-grading of the tied estate has led the industry to invest well in excess of £1,000 million in the past decade and a half. Despite this, the major brewers' 'performance' record has been criticised, notably in the recent Price Commission Report. Two issues in particular have attracted attention. One is the suggestion that the big brewers are 'inefficient' compared with their smaller competitors as indicated by their lower profitability. (Had they made higher profits then they would presumably have been charged with 'abusing' their market power!) The second concerns the discrepancy between the rates of return earned by the brewers (both large and small alike) on the production side of their businesses as compared with beer retailing. The Price Commission found that with regard to the rate of return on capital employed in brewing and wholesaling the larger brewers had a much lower return (32 per cent on average) than either the regional (46 per cent) or the small brewers (53 per cent). These figures in turn were considerably greater than the return on the tied estate which averaged a meagre 3 per cent for all three categories of firm. On the face of it this evidence seems to suggest that the large brewers' investment programmes have been 'inefficient' and that the brewers' tied business has been consistently 'unprofitable'.

With reference to the Price Commission's view that the large brewers achieved lower rates of return than either regional or small firms the first point which needs to be made is that investment is deemed to be undertaken to obtain a satisfactory rate of return on capital rather than to increase profit margins on sales. If large firms do earn lower rates of return on capital than small firms, that should not be taken as evidence of inefficient investment without analysing its causes. A firm which is behaving optimally from the viewpoint of its owners will increase its investment so long as each increment earns a rate of return in excess of the cost of capital. However, it is important to remember that the accounting ratio of profit to capital employed is intended to approximate the *average* rate of return over all projects. The firm which behaves optimally according to investment appraisal theory will not maximise its average rate of return — maximum rate of return would be achieved only by resticiting investment to a small set of highly profitable projects. Similarly, a firm which optimises investment and output decisions will not maximise its profit *margin* — a maximum profit margin would be obtained by restricting output. Consequently, the observation that small firms earn higher rates of return and higher margins

— if valid — might be explained by their having different investment policies compared to larger firms. Diversification by larger firms may well lead to lower average rates of return commensurate with lower levels of firm risk. Small firms may have decided to restrict their investment levels, either because they lack the managerial resources to control larger operations or because capital markets operate in a way which restricts the ability of small firms to obtain finance. Another possibility is that small firms apply sub-optimal methods of investment appraisal leading to the rejection of marginally worthwhile projects. All such possible explanations of differences in achieved rates of return would have to be investigated before any firm conclusions could be reached regarding their significance.

Secondly, it is well known that conventional accounting methods may produce misleading measures of rates of return on capital employed. The Price Commission itself admitted that calculations of earnings on capital employed based on balance sheet values 'need to be treated with a considerable degree of scepticism'.[15] Unfortunately, the Commission then largely ignored this cautionary comment and emphasised the significance of comparative rates of return without attempting to quantify the amount or direction of bias in the figures being analysed. All schemes for inter-firm comparisons must clearly define the level of profits (for example, operating profit plus increases in property values) and the level of total or net assets. A particularly important question is whether small firms have revalued their assets more or less recently than large firms and whether there is consequently a systematic distortion between the measured rates of return of the two groups. Two companies carrying out similar activities with equal efficiency will disclose different accounting rates of return if one carries its assets at their original cost whereas the other revalues them in line with current prices.[16] With regard to Table 5.5 the three large companies, Allied Breweries, Bass Charrington and Whitbread carried out revaluations in 1972, 1973 and 1974-5; Greenall Whitley also revalued in 1973. By contrast Wolverhampton and Dudley, which shows the largest rate of return, carries all property at cost. This company's accounts disclose that in 1976 its properties had a value £16 million higher than the balance sheet indicated, and if this 'surplus' had been included the rate of return would have fallen from 23.5 per cent to 13 per cent. Matthew Brown and Davenport had not revalued most of their property since 1964 and 1965. This factor alone suggests that any apparent excess of return earned by the small companies over that earned by the large firms is almost certainly attributable to the effect of their valuation

Table 5.5 Ratio analysis of accounting reports on eight firms: 1970-76

	Profit: equity capital		Profit and interest Equity and loans		Profit and interest: sales		Stocks: sales		Sales growth % p.a. (average)	Current depreciation: profit	
	1970	1976	1970	1976	1970	1976	1970	1976		1970	1976
Allied	11.7	14.5	9.6	12.0	10.8	8.8	14.9	18.6	21.6	18.5	31.2
Bass Charrington	11.4	16.1	10.5	14.9	11.3	11.1	10.5	12.1	22.1	13.3	25.2
Whitbread	8.8	12.9	6.0	11.2	10.0	10.5	9.3	12.7	26.8	19.1	24.6
Greenall Whitley	10.2	13.5	10.0	13.0	11.7	11.6	8.6	7.0	27.5	16.1	22.5
Wolverhampton & Dudley	18.3	23.5	17.1	23.4	14.7	15.1	8.3	8.8	26.8	13.7	17.5
Matthew Brown	11.2	16.2	10.4	16.3	20.4	17.8	5.7	5.7	21.6	6.7	14.6
Davenport	16.5	17.4	14.6	16.7	7.6	7.6	13.1	8.3	N.A.	22.4	29.5
John Young	14.5	13.7	12.8	12.7	N.A.	10.1	6.8	11.4	20.7	17.7	20.2

Source: Company Balance Sheets.

policies. All the firms in Table 5.5 and nearly all those in Table 5.6 were included in the Price Commission's survey. Once allowance is made for the unrealistic valuations of assets noted above, the differences in rates of return between the large brewers and the smaller firms become far less significant than in the Price Commission's analysis. Indeed Table 5.6 suggests that the large firms have a clear advantage.

Table 5.6 Return on capital employed for selected firms, 1968-74

| | Pre-Interest profits as % of capital employed | | | |
	1968	1971	1974	Property revalued
Large firms				
Allied	11.0	13.1	13.6	1973
Bass Charrington	9.2	12.9	11.5	1973
Whitbread	8.3	10.2	7.5	1974
Guinness	20.0	22.6	14.8	1973
Scottish & Newcastle	12.6	16.1	10.8	1974
Average	12.2	14.9	11.6	
Regional firms				
Cameron	13.4	15.9	10.1	1974
Greenall Whitley	7.8	12.3	9.1	1974
Greene King	12.7	15.2	16.3	Not revalued
Vaux	9.4	11.9	12.8	Not revalued
Average	10.8	13.8	12.0	
Small firms				
Boddington	13.0	14.1	18.8	Not revalued
Mansfield	18.3	21.3	22.6	Not revalued
Tollemache Cobbold	5.8	7.4	6.4	Not revalued
Higson	15.0	19.3	11.0	1974
Average	13.0	15.5	14.7	

Source: Company Balance Sheets.

N.B. On the assumption that a revaluation of assets which have not been revalued for at least 20 years will reduce the rate of return by a conservative 50%, the 1974 figure for Greene King would be 8.1% and for Vaux 6.4%, bringing the average return for the regional group down to 7.9%. The same reduction applied to the small group would bring their average down to 8.7%. Even if Guinness is excluded from the large brewers' sample, their average rate for 1974 would still be 10.8%.

Some of the regional and small firms shown above do in fact revalue their property on a regular basis, but the increase in value is not reflected in their balance sheet data.

Thirdly, the Commission laid considerable emphasis on the apparently low return from the tied estate compared with that on brewing and wholesaling. The Brewers' Society had in fact argued before the

Monopolies Commission that it would be illogical and misleading to apportion capital employed between different sections of a vertically-integrated industry. The Society pointed out that such an approach would lead to presenting relatively high returns on beer, varying returns on wines and spirits, and negligible returns on licensed premises and that it would be erroneous to conclude from this that the level of profits on beer was too high and that its return on licensed premises was so low that the industry could not be making effective use of its resources. The point was that tied houses (and loans to the free trade) were an integral part of a brewery's production, distribution and selling operations and therefore the return on capital employed must be evaluated across the whole enterprise, not merely in one section of it. The Monopolies Commission accepted this argument and, indeed, has applied the same integral approach to at least one investigation in another, similar industry.[17] The Price Commission, however, summarily brushed this objection aside on the grounds that the brewers' preferred method of calculating the return on the business as a whole 'obscures the very high return on brewing and enables them to contend that returns of the order of 9 per cent and 10 per cent are modest in comparison with industry generally'.[18] Yet why should the brewers — or anyone else — have invested so heavily in an asset with such a low rate of return if it were not for the fact that it provides them with an outlet for their products? If the tied house system were abolished, the situation would not change very much since most brewers would then become much more heavily committed to their loan business in the free trade. In its apportionment, the Price Commission classed free trade loans with the tied estate and implied that the return from such loans was as low as that from licensed houses. Yet the loan tie must be seen in exactly the same context as the ownership tie, in other words, as a method of securing an outlet for production. It is therefore absurd to place a separate value on it. Yet the Commission accused the brewers of adopting an approach to investment and deployment of funds which was 'quite outmoded'. The Commission thus appears to have formed the impression that simply because the brewers do not consider that a calculation of the return on capital invested in the tied estate is meaningful, they are unable to evaluate the returns on that investment for decision purposes. Correct investment appraisal, however, does not require an arbitrary allocation of profits between one activity and another, but a valuation of expected total income with and without a particular asset.

In any case, the Commission to some extent contradicted itself by implying that the brewers were keeping the return on their tied estate artificially low. The brewers valued their tied property 'on the basis of a multiple of expected profit', and the Commission took exception to this method:

> Where assets are revalued to reflect the change in the market value of the property, this produces a true measure of the capital actually invested in the business . . . But where assets are revalued to reflect anticipated earning power, the increase in value does not in any sense represent capital which has been invested in the business . . . the level of profit earned will do little more than reflect the level of profit assumed. If a low rate is assumed, the level of earnings will be low; and periodic revaluation will ensure that the disclosed level of earnings is kept down to the level postulated.[19]

This distinction between market value and earnings potential is, however, a curious one. Market values should in fact reflect the earnings potential of the assets concerned; earnings potential is surely the ultimate justification for holding assets and market prices will adjust through competitive pressures to levels which enable purchasers to obtain reasonable rates of return. The difficulty with licensed property lies not in the method of valuation but in the fact that some assets are revalued whilst others are not, and that different firms undertake revaluations at different times.

The brewers' rejection of the concept of sectional returns on capital does not mean that every tied house is retained indefinitely, regardless of its profitability or scope for future development, merely because it provides an outlet for a firm's beer. Indeed, it can be argued that the most radical change engendered, or at least greatly accelerated by the formation of the national groups has been in the management of licensed property. It was argued in Chapter 2 that one major effect of the 1904 Act and the compensation procedure was to encourage brewery companies to retain licensed houses which, on strictly commercial criteria, should have been closed. The consequences of the licensing laws and the restrictive way in which local justices interpreted them were quickly rationalised within the general philosophy of 'social responsibility' which pervaded the industry between the wars. The normative influence of this concept survived well into the post-war period. As Seldon observed in the early 1950s:

> A brewing business is a colony of houses; to close one is to abandon a member of the colony, and so the strong support the weak. Business decisions which have salutary but harsh consequences cannot, moreover, be taken lightly by men who are prominent in

local life. Nor is it easy to deal on strictly business lines with public houses that are not merely multiple shops but also traditional centres of social life, and whose tenants are also local figures.[20]

Or, as the managing director of Courage Barclay observed in 1958:

The brewer is very conscious that the licensed house is in fact part of the national life and there are times when profit or loss cannot be the main consideration. I can say with assurance that there is not a brewery company in the whole of the country which does not own in greater or lesser degree a number of houses which are being carried on at a loss, having no prospect of making a profit, but are kept open to meet a local need.[21]

As the ownership of licensed houses became concentrated in fewer hands, however, this attitude became less influential. The growing demand for improved amenities in public houses also challenged the traditional view. Thus it was noted:

Small independent breweries have difficulty in competing in the rush to make their premises more attractive to customers and to provide those additional amenities essential in an increasingly competitive business. A brewer with a limited number of tied houses may be convinced of the necessity of keeping all his houses in existence, but a merger with another concern may alter the property position quite sharply, permitting the closure of previously competing houses and allowing the proceeds to be spent on modernising other, or if the site sold was a valuable one, the building of a new house in a more profitable area.[22]

In Birmingham both Mitchells and Butlers and Ansell had pursued a policy of 'fewer and better' since the 1920s, and they had been encouraged to do so not merely by a sympathetic licensing bench but also by the fact that between them they almost monopolised the tied trade in the city and were thus in a position to cooperate closely in the selection of redundant houses and the construction of new ones. This degree of cooperation, however, was exceptional, and taking the industry as a whole a major advance in this field could not be achieved until the ownership of licensed houses was much more concentrated. It was no accident, therefore, that during the 1950s it was the largest property owner — Ind Coope and Allsopp — who led the way in rationalising licensed property. Between 1958 and 1961 the company realised £9 millions from the sale of properties and in 1959-60 alone sold no fewer than 430 licensed outlets. As the major groups emerged during the 1960s, so they all began to re-appraise their assets and large numbers of houses were either closed or sold to private buyers. Between 1968 and 1973 Whitbread alone closed or sold about 300 houses each year.

It was noted in a previous chapter that some of the 'improved public houses' built between the wars were relatively unprofitable investments for brewery companies, at least in the short-term. The problem of low returns continued into the post-war period. As Simon Combe, the chairman of Watney Combe and Reid, observed in 1955: 'It is a matter of growing concern that the tremendous expenditure on new houses, and on the rebuilding and improvement of existing houses, does little more than conserve turnover and as an investment produces no additional return'. Taken at its face value, this statement would appear to reinforce the Price Commission's argument. Yet it must be remembered that each new, improved house frequently replaced more than one older house and that up to the mid-1950s the overall consumption of beer was declining. Consequently one would not have expected these new houses to do much more than conserve existing turnover. When, however, consumption began to rise and the opportunities for growth in the on-licensed trade became much more evident, the brewers adopted a new approach to the management of their property assets. Some houses which were thought to have no future in relation to the total operations of a firm were put up for sale. Others which were either newly built or had been greatly improved were put under direct management.[23] As noted above, however, the main emphasis was on giving tenants a greater incentive to increase their trade. Consequently property rents became more realistic and 'wet rent' was abolished. It should be emphasised once again that the brewers' efforts to improve the profitability of their tied estates were matched and complemented by their efforts to raise the productivity of the assets employed in production and distribution. In short, one must regard post-merger rationalisation as designed to improve the use of resources throughout the industry, not simply in one part of it.

It may, however, be argued that even allowing for un-revalued assets, the advantage held by the large brewers represented in Table 5.6 is not as impressive as one might have expected, given all the advantages that are supposed to flow from large-scale production and national distribution. To the extent that this point has substance, it must be remembered that the rate of concentration in the brewing industry since 1958 is attributable almost entirely to merger activity. Empirical studies of the relationship between mergers and profitability in a variety of industries both in Britain and the USA do not, however, suggest that the relationship is in general a positive one. Indeed, most studies to date suggest that mergers either lead to a lower level of profitability or else have a neutral effect.[24] In a recent analysis of the performance of a group of merger-intensive firms in British manufacturing industry relative to that of a control group of other firms, Utton concluded that

> . . . companies heavily dependent on external expansion may, in a subsequent period of largely internal growth, pay the price of lower overall efficiency (to the extent that this is reflected in their rate of return on net assets), than companies whose long term growth is slower but whose internal efficiency can be sustained . . . perhaps for as long as five years after an acquisition or series of acquisitions the full effects of reorganisation and adjustment are making themselves felt on profitability.[25]

There is no reason to suppose that the national brewery groups were any less prone to post-merger readjustment problems than the firms in Utton's sample. Thus one early (1964) survey of the performance of merger-intensive breweries relative to that of other firms underlined the slowness with which the benefits of mergers were being realised. The author found that five large groups had increased their properties by an average of 69 per cent over the preceding five years and had seen their equity earnings rise by 39.5 per cent. By contrast, nineteen smaller firms who had increased their properties by an average of 26 per cent saw their equity earnings rise by 49 per cent. The difference was attributed to the fact that the large groups had paid too much for their acquisitions, though, as argued earlier, this argument must be treated with caution.[26] In some cases, however, the process of integration was certainly retarded by political and organisational difficulties.[27] Indeed, in view of the fact that at the present time most of the national groups are still engaged in rationalising their production capacity and constructing new plant, it could be argued that the full advantages of large-scale operation will not be seen until the early years of the next decade.[28] The point which must be emphasised, however, is that any shortcomings in the performance of the national groups cannot be attributed to vertical integration as such since the groups themselves were formed through a series of horizontal mergers. The advantages of expanding through acquisition in order to achieve national coverage must be seen in terms of horizontal market power; any disadvantages arising from national status must therefore be seen in the same terms. The approach of the Price Commission, which attributed the allegedly poor relative performance of the large brewers to vertical integration, is rejected.

The Industry and the Consumer

A number of criticisms relating to the issue of consumer sovereignty have been raised in connection with the tied public house system and the brewers' recent pursuit of economies in production, distribution and marketing. These include complaints about the limitation of choice, the quality and strength of 'modern' beers and the character of the English public house.

Let us begin by looking first at the contention that the tied house system has 'unduly' restricted consumer choice. When considering this matter, it must be recognised that there is a potential conflict in any industry between, on the one hand, achieving economies of scale and capacity production by concentrating on a small number of standardised lines, and, on the other hand, supplying a sufficient variety of brands to satisfy the diverse tastes of consumers. As a 'batch' rather than a 'continuous flow' production industry, the scope in brewing for achieving economies through standardisation is limited. Indeed, in the past the industry has been criticised for producing too many different brands of beer; certainly the merger boom of 1959-62 does not appear to have resulted in product rationalisation on a significant scale.[29] As late as 1966 the brewers were still producing approximately 3,000 different brands. The N.B.P.I. argued that production could be made more economical through a reduction in the number of brands, and that this would in turn facilitate the introduction of new manufacturing techniques. It also asserted, however, that a reduced range of beers would not necessarily restrict the consumer's choice in view of the growing importance of reciprocal trading.[30] Although the Board offered no quantitive evidence in support of its argument, the brewers appear to have acted upon it and by 1976 the total number of brands produced had been cut to 1,500.[31] The problem of choice, however, is rather more complex than the N.B.P.I. suggested. Two separate issues are involved: firstly, what is a 'reasonable' range of choice in a particular public house, and secondly, how many public houses and other licensed premises offering different ranges of beers are there in a particular locality?

It is inevitable that brewer ownership of licensed houses involves some limitation on the range of brands available in a given tied outlet. The following considerations should, however, be borne in mind when assessing the reasonableness of this limitation. Firstly, the size of most houses means that there are definite physical limits on the number and range of products which can be stocked there. Secondly, licensees who sell draught beer (especially in its traditional form) need to achieve a reasonably rapid turnover of stock in order to maintain the quality of their brands. Thirdly, licensees are acutely conscious of the economies of retailing, which tend towards the smallest range of products compatible with serving the needs of customers and avoid the 'locking up' of large amounts of working capital in slow-moving stock. The fact that these considerations apply as much to free trade licensees suggests that if the tied house system did not exist there would still be only a limited range of brands available in any one outlet. Indeed, it seems likely, as the Brewers' Society told the Monopolies Commission, that in a free market many licensees would 'play safe' and stock only national brands, thereby removing some of the diversity which the tied house system guarantees. It must also be recognised that 'choice' is a normative concept and hence difficult to quantify by any objective yardstick. Given the constraints noted above, it seems that the range of beers typically offered in a tied house is, at least for most consumers, not unreasonable. A survey conducted by the Brewers' Society and submitted to the Commission suggested that at that time a majority of houses offered two draught beers, four bottled light ales, two brown ales, two stouts, one keg beer and one lager. In wines and spirits the consumer usually had a choice between well-known national brands and the brewer's own house brands. The Society did not deny that a free house would tend to sell the products of perhaps two or three different brewers, but pointed out that the total range of products on offer might be no wider than in a tied house.

In any event it could be argued that it is immaterial whether the consumer exercises his choice at one outlet (tied or otherwise) or at a number of outlets in a given locality. Provided customers have reasonable access to the public houses of competing brewers, their choice opportunities need not be impaired. The Brewers' Society argued that mergers, the growth of free trade outlets, reciprocal trading and advertising had all combined to enable brewers to penetrate regional markets where previously they had no base:

> The fact is that every area of the UK is now open to a brewer who has the financial and technical resources to market his beers in that area, provided only that they are acceptable to consumers in that area. The tied house system has not prevented, and cannot prevent, the consequence of these developments.[32]

The Society carried out an extensive enquiry for the Commission which showed that in most areas there was a wide range of beers available.[33] This was endorsed by the Commission who agreed that apart from a number of local monopolies it was the case that in nearly all urban areas there were public houses owned by several different brewers within close proximity of one another.[34] In addition, of course, the range of choice between places to drink and between the products of different brewers is considerably greater than this when account is taken of non-tied outlets. In fact, since the Commission reported not only has the brewers' tied trade declined relative to the free trade but even in those few areas where a high concentration of ownership by one brewer existed (for example, Bristol, Norwich and Birmingham) firms have subsequently exchanged public houses with each other to broaden their representation.[35]

As noted earlier, the post-merger rationalisation programmes of the major brewers has inevitably led to the replacement of some local beers by national brands and a substantial investment in public house improvements. These changes have not always been to the liking of 'traditionalists' who have charged the brewers with purveying 'gassy and weak' keg beers and lager and with destroying the character of the English public house. What truth is there in these allegations?

Keg beers and lager have been variously condemned for being too 'pressurised', too 'standardised' and 'flavourless'. This type of beer, according to one critic 'provides for the average taste of the North and South, of men and women, young and old.'[36] There is no doubt that keg beer and lager do appeal to a large and broad cross-section of drinkers (see Table 3.3, p. 56); if they did not it would be difficult to account for their growing popularity over the past decade. It should be noted, however, that the apparent convergence of taste around a norm is not a new phenomenon. The demand for light, sparkling beer of relatively moderate gravity first began to emerge well over a century ago, and was a key factor underlying the enormous success of the Burton brewers. From the 1920s onwards this convergence of taste was reflected in the growing demand for bottled beer which by the 1950s accounted for over one-half of total beer sales. Significantly, keg beer started to grow in popularity as bottled beer began to lose its market share and given the similarity between the two products one might suggest that many of the drinkers who switched to keg beer during the 1960s were former drinkers of bottled beer. Thus, market trends indicate that ever since the First World War a significant and growing section of the drinking population has expressed a preference for clear, sparkling, filtered and pasteurised beer. Until the early 1960s this demand was met by bottled beer and since then keg and lager have captured this sector of the market.[37]

It is true that most beers nowadays are much lower in alcoholic strength than they were last century. Beer gravities were first reduced at the Government's request during the First World War and a combination of factors including rising raw material costs, higher rates of excise duty and the pronounced swing in consumer demand towards lighter beers, have served to reduce them further. Moreover, public attitudes towards drink have changed and with them the idea that drinking to get drunk has steadily gone out of fashion. To this extent the alcoholic content of beer has seemed to matter less. Since 1970, however, the gravities of many premium beers have in fact been increased. *Worthington E*, for example, which had an original gravity of about 1037° in 1970 now has an original gravity of 1040°.[38]

Alcoholic content, however, is only one of a number of factors making up the 'quality' of a beer. The other factors include character (fullness, bitterness, aroma), consistency, brilliance, head retention and gas content. Different people look for different things in a glass of beer and once the complexities of individual taste are fully recognised it becomes increasingly difficult to accept broad generalisations which imply that most people would prefer to drink only traditional draught beer or, for that matter, bottled or keg beer. To suggest that the big brewery groups would really like to dispense with traditional draught beer altogether is patently absurd.[39]

In addition to destroying the traditional character of English beer, the major brewers are also alleged to be 'vandalising' the English public house. According to Hutt:

> The pub that millions know and love is being wrecked, deliberately, willfully. The brewers are the vandals. The only real difference between them and the people who paint slogans on walls and tear up flowers in the park, is that the brewers will not be in court on Monday morning to answer for their actions.[40]

Once again, however, the problem needs to be put in perspective. We have discussed earlier the brewers' attempts, during the inter-war years, to stem falling sales by improving their public houses. Overall these efforts were clearly inadequate and many public houses continued to remain uninviting in appearance and lacking in facilities. Progress in improving houses was slow partly because of financial constraints and the opposition of justices, but more fundamentally it was due to the fact that the industry's main customers were not interested in change. Most public houses relied heavily on a male, working-class clientele which demanded relatively little in the way of amenities, furnishings and decor.

From the 1950s onwards, however, tastes and expectations began to change. A younger, more affluent generation of drinkers, an increasing proportion of whom were women, would not tolerate the former level of amenities in public houses. Growing recognition of the fact that the brewing trade in general, and the public house as a social institution in particular, were part of a wider, rapidly expanding leisure industry complex not only led the brewers to adopt a more critical attitude toward running their businesses but also to a massive investment in public house improvements. Houses were extensively modernised and redesigned, and better comforts and sanitary facilities provided. Publicans were increasingly encouraged to offer food and restaurant facilities as well as a wider range of entertainments. Without question this improvement programme has been a resounding success as may be guaged from the fact that the steady drift away from the public house has been halted and reversed. More people, representing a wider cross-section of society, are 'regular' public house visitors than ever before. In the process, of course, it was inevitable that certain features of public house life would disappear, most notably in some cases the traditional 'spit-and-sawdust' tap-room and the 'Victorian' lounge or saloon bar, but it would be remarkable indeed if every improvement had managed to satisfy all tastes. To suggest, as 'traditionalists' do, that these new tendencies are in some way perverse or represent a 'retreat' from what a public house ought to be is invalid, for as the Erroll Committee has noted:

> It is impossible to generalise about the public house. Everyone has his own ideal image. For some, the term conjures up a vision of an old country town coaching inn; for others it may mean a small village pub, a city discotheque or a dockland bar. *It makes little sense to commit oneself to a particular view of what should constitute a public house.* They tend to reflect the social tastes and requirements of a particular neighbourhood and the extent to which people are prepared to pay for these. Thus the sort of facilities which people find attractive in Ascot and Sunningdale would be entirely out of place in the middle of a large provincial city or an industrial area.[41]

Within this framework, however, the Erroll Committee reported that it had detected '. . . a general trend towards public houses with an increasing number of facilities for refreshments and leisure'.

6 The Industry, 'Workable Competition', and the Public Interest

In the introduction to this study four questions were posed concerning the structure, conduct and performance of the brewing industry. The purpose of this concluding section is to summarise our findings on the first three and to discuss the fourth, i.e. the policy options which now confront the State as the ultimate arbiter of the licensing laws.

The Evolution of the Market Structure

It will be remembered that the structure of any market embraces factors such as the degree of seller and buyer concentration, the degree of product differentiation, and conditions of entry into the market. In the case of the brewing industry the key characteristics are vertical integration and high barriers to entry, both of which emerged at a relatively early stage, and horizontal concentration, which is a more recent development. Product differentiation has also played a strategic role in the evolution of the market structure, although in recent years its importance has diminished significantly.

The Monopolies Commission's Report contains only the most cursory discussion of the historical development of forward integration by the brewers into retailing and strongly infers that restrictive licensing was almost entirely to blame. It has been argued in this study, however, that this is at best only a half-truth. The introduction of stringent controls on the issue of new retail licences in 1869 was certainly followed by a rapid contraction in the free sector of the market, but it seems highly probable that other factors besides restrictive licensing were involved. Firstly, it would appear that outside London and Burton, brewery ownership of licensed houses was widespread, at least in urban areas, *before* the onset of restrictive licensing. Many provincial firms tended to own houses within easy reach of their breweries for practical economic reasons, namely the perishability of their product and the need to exercise technical supervision over its sale and management once it was in the publican's hands. Secondly, in so far as there was a competitive scramble between provincial firms to buy licensed houses this did not develop until the late 1880s and early 1890s, or in other words until well over a decade *after* the new restrictions had been introduced. In general, the spread of tied trade in the provinces appears to have proceeded fairly gradually up to the second half of the 1880s, when the boom in company floatations signalled the beginning of a more intensive period of property acquisition. Even then, some firms were reluctant buyers of licensed houses and only entered the market in self-defence. The London and Burton brewers, by contrast, did not begin to buy property until the last decade of the century, when the drift of political opinion was moving decisively in favour of an enforced reduction in the number of houses. This evidence therefore casts doubt on the traditional argument that the growth of the tied house system was largely or exclusively the result of restrictive licensing.

The real spur to forward integration during the last two decades of the century was the marked decline in the level of demand for beer. The rapid expansion of demand during the mid-Victorian era had encouraged many firms to increase their productive capacity to a point where guaranteed retail outlets became a necessity once it became clear that the anticipated rate of growth would not be realised. In the larger urban areas the fall in demand meant that the number of retail outlets was excessive in relation to the volume of sales, hence the breakdown of the loan-tie in London and the growing problem of the 'long-pull'. Both the London and the Burton brewers found that the loan-tie gave them insufficient market security in a period of severe competition. Belatedly and reluctantly, these firms began to compete with each other in buying the leases of licensed houses and in simultaneously offering bigger loans to publicans. The financial implications of forward integration in turn led them to issue large quantities of debenture stock to the public. In most cases, however, the rationale of property acquisition was essentially defensive. Many firms, both in London and the provinces, found themselves having to buy houses with which they had customarily traded on a free or loan-tie basis simply in order to defend their existing volume of sales. As the joint stock boom developed, so the brewers gained access to additional funds for property acquisition, competitive buying increased, and the market value of licensed houses rose sharply. It is hardly coincidental, however, that the property boom of 1894-99 was accompanied by a marked though temporary recovery in the level of demand which undoubtedly helped to revive the old feeling of optimism about the industry's prospects. Indeed, without this optimism it would be difficult to explain the remarkable willingness of investors to buy brewery stocks and shares. It is also significant, in view of the importance conventionally attached to restrictive licensing, that this optimism does not appear to have been diminished in any way by the law lords' decisions in *Sharpe v Wakefield* reaffirming the justices' right to remove licences on the grounds of superfluity. In the early 1900s, however, the market entered a prolonged recession and property values, especially in London, had to be severely written down. In the provinces, where the inflation of property values had been less severe, the period of readjustment was correspondingly less painful and several firms continued to extend their tied estates by acquiring other companies. The fact that they did so at a time when both local licensing justices and Parliament were setting about the task of closing public houses strengthens the conclusion advanced above, namely that the key factor in the growth of tied trade was the level of demand. Restrictive licensing certainly reinforced the logic of forward integration yet, bearing in mind all the uncertainties surrounding the security of licensed property in the period 1900-14 (which were by no means entirely removed by the 1904 Act), the possession of a public house did not at this time guarantee a secure outlet. After 1904 the licensing system as such contributed to the growth of tied trade only to the extent that some firms may have decided that the bigger their property holdings were, the less they would feel the loss of any houses referred for compensation.

Vertical integration was, therefore, implicit in the very nature of beer retailing and the speed with which it advanced between about 1886 and 1900 was primarily a reflection of the level of demand. Horizontal integration, by contrast, developed much more slowly. The degree of concentration which the London brewers had achieved before 1830 did not become general throughout the country as a whole until the 1960s. This fragmentation is commonly attributed to the tied house system. The conventional argument is that tied trade gave small and middle-sized firms enough security to enable them to make adequate profits and survive, even in a market which, after 1900, was contracting fairly steadily. While there is a large measure of truth in this view, the situation is in reality more complex. In the period 1888-1902, for example, many manufacturing industries witnessed a sharp increase in merger activity in response to excessive price competition. In the brewing industry, by contrast, price competition as such was not so important and the incentive to merge for defensive reasons — at least in this early period — was correspondingly weaker. When the market for beer moved into its long period of decline, the logic of concentration as a method of eliminating surplus productive capacity became much more compelling. The fact that progress was still slower than one might have expected is attributable to the pervasive influence of family ownership and control, and the continuing importance of local tastes and preferences in the retail market, as well as to the tied house system. As long as cask beer remained the industry's staple product, there was no reason why small local firms should not continue to sell their draught beer through their tied houses for as long as the controlling family wanted to carry on the business. When, for whatever reason, the family decided to sell out, the normal course of action was for them to initiate discussions with a larger firm whose tied trade lay adjacent to, or overlapped with, their own. There is no evidence to suggest that this practice was peculiar to the brewing industry at this time. The idea of competitive or uninvited bidding was still quite alien to British industry in general. In this 'golden age of directorial power', the initiative lay with the small family groups and their friends who controlled the majority of firms both inside and outside the brewing industry. Nevertheless, the pattern of merger activity during the inter-war period reveals a tendency for some firms to seek regional status and to this extent it may be said that they were more willing to receive offers from small companies, and perhaps even to initiate discussions themselves, than other firms. Without the active support of the directors of a 'victim' firm, however, even the most ambitious company would not proceed to make an offer. The influence of family interests was again evident in the slowness with which post-merger rationalisation frequently proceeded, and it was often several years before the brand names and public house signs of an acquired company disappeared. This cautious approach to rationalisation could also be justified, however, in terms of the need to retain the goodwill of an acquired firm's traditional customers.

Since the 1950s some of these constraints on horizontal integration have lost their force. The first and most important factor has been the growth of a national market for beer. While a national market first emerged with the development of the railway network from 1840-75, it remained largely the preserve of a small number of London and Burton brewers from the 1890s until the late 1950s. It was also confined mainly to the sale, through reciprocal trading agreements and the free trade, of a restricted range of well-known bottled beers. The national market expanded during the 1950s as the demand for bottled beer increased and reciprocal trading became more and more widespread. Indeed, many small firms came to rely on national and regional firms for their supplies of bottled beer. The development of keg and 'pressurised' beers, however, implied a fundamental challenge to the market position of locally-brewed cask beer. The need to improve the standard of amenities in tied houses posed a further challenge to many small firms. During the inter-war years it became increasingly evident that licensed houses could no longer be regarded as mere drink shops. During the 1950s the spread of television ownership, and in the following decade the rapid growth of competitive leisure facilities, implied that if the public house was to survive, enormous investment would be needed in order to change its image and attract new customers. Rather than confront this challenge with inadequate resources, many small to middle-sized firms decided to sell out. The merger boom of 1959-62 was, of course, precipitated by the activities of 'outsiders', and once it had got under way it developed its own momentum so that (as in the property boom of the 1890s) the predominant influence behind many decisions was the fear of being 'left out in the cold'. Nevertheless, the growth of the national market and the competitive pressure to improve tied houses were the two underlying factors which together accelerated the process of horizontal integration. Both these developments were in turn a function of the changing character of consumer demand. The conclusion must be, therefore, that while the tied house system may have helped to retard the process of concentration in the past, it has not proved to be an impregnable defence against those changes in the character of demand which have in recent years encouraged the formation of a small number of national brewery groups.

The rapid growth of the national market has also diminished the significance of product differentiation. Up to the 1960s, however, product differentiation played an important role in shaping the character of competition within the industry. The most extreme example of continued growth through product differentiation is Guinness, which has never entered the licensed property market in the UK and thus remains the only brewery company which is not directly involved in retailing. The rapid growth of the Burton trade during the mid-Victorian era was also based on product differentiation in so far as the market position of the Burton brewers (especially Bass and Allsopp) depended on the unique quality of their pale ales. The popularity of Burton beer broke the monopoly of porter in the London market and compelled brewers in both London and the provinces to imitate its characteristics. By the 1880s it was clear that many firms had succeeded in doing so, and it was this factor as much as the growth of the tied house system which brought Burton's remarkable period of growth to an end. It could be argued with some justice that the contraction of the free, national market which occurred as a result of the extension of the tied house system after 1880 tended to consolidate local tastes and thereby reinforced product differentiation. It certainly helped to squeeze ' some provincial firms out of their more distant markets. Nevertheless, the goodwill which the larger firms in Burton had built up behind their brands enabled them to continue to distribute their main beers more or less nationally even though none of them had anything approaching national coverage in the tied trade. The growth of bottled beer sales during the inter-war period encouraged some of the major London brewers to market their main brands over a wide area beyond London, principally through reciprocal trading. This strategy was maintained until well into the 1950s, and was pursued with particular vigour by Whitbread's. Indeed, until the late 1950s there was still a sharp differentiation in terms of price and quality between locally brewed cask beer and nationally or regionally-brewed bottled beer. The development of keg beer (which was, in effect, bottled beer in draught form) increasingly blurred this division, however, and both encouraged and reflected a general convergence of taste. The characteristics of keg beer and lager suggest that consumers are now much more prepared to substitute one brand for another. In this sense the growth of a national market is symptomatic of the declining importance of product differentiation, as well as being itself a contributory factor in that decline.

The final key element in the industry's market structure is the barrier against new entrants. The conventional argument is that the tied house system has not only given each of the brewers a protected market for their products but has given the industry as a whole a high degree of protection against competition from external sources. At best, however, this is only a half-truth. In the London trade prior to the 1890s, brewery ownership of licensed houses was (except for a short period during the French wars) exceptional and played a far less significant role in the retail trade than the loan-tie. Yet entry into the market itself was still very difficult because the metropolitan brewers had already achieved the economies of large-scale production. Consequently any new entrant would have had to face the enormous capital costs of setting up a large brewery which could compete in costs of production and quality of output with those of the established firms, leaving aside the cash balance required for entering the loan trade. Those new entrants who did penetrate the London trade to a significant degree from the 1840s onwards were, firstly, the major Bruton brewers whose competitive strength was derived from the product they sold and, secondly, the smaller firms on the old perimeter of London who became part of the real metropolitan trade as the city itself spread outwards. These firms, together with several smaller brewers based in the provinces, sought to enter the London market primarily because up to the 1870s it was exceptionally large and expanding rapidly. When this growth phase came to an end during the 1870s, to be followed by a decade of declining demand, all those brewers who competed in the London market, indigenous and 'foreign' alike, were seriously affected. It was the increasing severity of competition between the London and Burton brewers for the loan trade which effectively drove the smaller provincial firms out of the market. When the London brewers actually began to buy licensed houses in the mid-1890s, the metropolitan trade had in effect been closed to new entrants for nearly twenty years.

It cannot, of course be denied that once the dominance of the tied house system was an established fact — as it was by the 1890s — any aspiring entrant was faced with the problem of buying virtually un-obtainable licensed houses. Yet he would also have been deterred by other factors, namely the lack of growth in the market and the capital costs of establishing new production facilities. During the mid-Victorian era the industry remained open to 'classic' entry primarily because the demand for beer was growing rapidly and 'cottage' scale production was still profitable. The liberal licensing policy which prevailed from 1830 until 1869 was also important in so far as it helped the brewers to ex-ploit the expanding urban market and enabled private individuals with little capital to enter the retail trade. The industry ceased to attract new entrants from the late 1870s onwards partly because the market had begun to decline and partly because the capital costs of entry had risen rapidly. The difficulty of obtaining new licences and the growing strength of the tied house system undoubtedly added to the difficulties facing new entrants, but these were not the only factors which made brewing a closed industry. From 1880 onwards 'classic' entry was un-likely to occur as long as the industry appeared to be in decline.[1] This situation prevailed until the early 1960s, when beer consumption moved into sustained growth and the issue of new off-licences was made much easier. This combination of rising demand and relatively liberal licensing encouraged small entrepreneurs to enter the retail trade. Entry into brewing itself, however, remained impossible except through take-overs, and these materialised when it became clear that the industry had considerable scope for future growth. Once the strategic role of the public house within a rapidly-growing leisure market was widely recognised, the tied house system — far from deterring new entrants — made the brewing industry an attractive proposition for firms with extensive interests in either the leisure market itself or in allied industries serving this market. The costs of entry have, of course, risen enormously since the 1950s due to a combination of factors, notably the growth of horizontal integration, the concentration of productive capacity in large new breweries, and the sustained increase in the value of licensed property. Nevertheless, the 'outsiders' who have entered the industry in recent years have obviously taken the view that the initial price of entry will ultimately be justified by the growth potential of brewing in particular and the leisure market in general.[2]

In conclusion, therefore, one can say that since the late 1950s the market structure has changed in several ways. Firstly, the degree of horizontal concentration has increased sharply. However, there is no dominant firm in the industry and the level of concentration has only been brought into line with the average for British manufacturing as a whole. Secondly, the relative importance of vertical integration has declined. The ownership of public houses is still a very important part of a brewery business, but the rapid growth of free trade outlets since 1961 has reduced the brewers' dependence on sales through their tied houses. In recent years the free trade has been the most dynamic sector of a growing market and the national brewers have, through the vigorous promotion of their national and regional brands, increased their sales to the point where this sector is nearly as important to them in volume terms as the tied trade. Thirdly, the growing importance of national brands has made product differentiation less significant than it has traditionally been. Finally, although the barriers to 'classic' entry into brewing itself have risen considerably over the past two decades, the traditional belief that the industry was permanently closed to 'outsiders' has been challenged by the entry of two large firms through take-overs. Barriers to entry exist in all oligopolistic, capital-intensive industries and there is no evidence to suggest that they are higher in brewing than in other comparable sectors. If the retail trade is considered separately, it must be recognised that in recent years this sector has been more open to entry by the small entrepreneur than at any time since 1869. All these changes in the market structure of the brewing industry are directly related to the reversal of the long secular decline in the demand for beer which has occurred over the past two decades. The partial liberalisation of the licensing system in 1961 and 1964 has undoubtedly encouraged the growth of demand but the system itself has never played the dominant role in determining the market structure that many observers have claimed for it.

Market Structure and Competition

The conventional view of the relationship between market structure and conduct in the industry emphasises the role of vertical integration in removing price competition from the retail trade. If this view is valid, one would expect to see a strong element of price competition in the period up to 1880 when vertical integration was by no means as comprehensive as it subsequently became. Price competition in its pure form, however, was never a serious factor in the retail trade. The price of beer was invariably fixed in relation to its quality and here, of course, there was a high level of competition. Both the premium brands of Burton beer and Guinness's stout were relatively expensive products and achieved rapid volume growth during the mid-Victorian era on the strength of their quality and reliability. In the provinces generally the dominant factor was the strength of local tastes and preferences and here again price was only significant in relation to the quality and characteristics of the product itself.

During the last quarter of the century, however, more and more country brewers began to produce their own 'Burton-type' pale and mild ales which under-cut Burton beer because of lower distribution costs. Competition from the country brewers, reinforced by the declining level of demand for beer in general, compelled the London and Burton brewers to cut their wholesale prices during the 1880s. The effectiveness of this policy, however, appears questionable. It was directed more at the publican than at the consumer and was designed to give him more incentive to take a given firm's beer. But it must also be seen as complementary to the large increases in loans to publicans advanced by the London and Burton brewers at this time. It was also in part a reaction to the spread of tied trade in the provinces. As Allsopp found to their cost, by the late 1880s it was no longer possible in a stagnant or declining market for any brewer, no matter how large or well-known, to rely exclusively on the quality of his product, and wholesale price competition in itself could do little to reverse the underlying trend in demand. The fact, however, that both Guinness and the large Burton brewers continued to take advantage of the tied house system after 1900 suggests that price relative to quality remained an important feature of competition in the retail trade.

Even if product differentiation had not been such a critical element in the retail market, it is by no means certain that there would have been a greater degree of price competition *per se*. The importance of price competition in any industry depends at least to some degree on the elasticity of demand, or in other words on the extent to which the demand for a particular product is sensitive to changes in its price. In the case of beer, retail prices were remarkably stable over the sixty-year period covering the mid-Victorian boom and the late Victorian/Edwardian recession. As noted above, the focus of competition in the retail trade was price relative to quality. During the period of declining demand up to 1914, competition also hinged on price relative to quantity (the 'long pull') but this did nothing to raise the overall level of demand. All that the long pull accomplished was to draw some trade from one outlet to another, and since most publicans soon resorted to the practice it quickly became self-defeating. In any case, the rigidity of beer prices was also a function of the level of duty, which from the 1880s onwards probably equalled the brewers' average wholesale profit per barrel. Price stability had important effects, however, on the level of demand for beer relative to that for certain other consumer goods. During the 1880s the sharp fall in the price of food made beer a relatively expensive commodity and produced a marked change in working-class spending habits. This development proved to be the fore-runner of the revolutionary change in the pattern of consumer spending which marked the inter-war years. Between 1920 and 1934 the price of beer fell far less than retail prices in general, and the real gains in purchasing power which many consumers enjoyed during this period were spent in ways which directly benefitted a new range of industries producing cheap durables for the mass market. It was not until the 1950s that relative prices moved back in favour of beer. Between 1947 and 1977 the general price level increased by some 550 per cent, whereas the increase in the retail price of alcoholic drink was only about 350 per cent. This movement in relative prices must have had some effect on the level of consumption, although this did not begin to show itself until the late 1950s.

Relative prices, however, were by no means the only factor which influenced the level of beer consumption over the long term. Short-term fluctuations in consumption might well be attributable to changes in the level of economic activity, in other words of wages and employment, which, at least up to 1940, tended to be regional or local in incidence. Over the longer term, however, the demand for beer depended not only on the amount of money which working class consumers had to spend, but also on their disposition to spend it, and this in turn was strongly influenced by social norms and habits. Up to the year 1914 drinking beer in public houses was a widespread and traditional feature of urban working class society. As a social habit, however, it owed its popularity to a combination of three factors — the squalor and overcrowding of the urban environment, the lack of alternative consumption goods, and the absence of competing leisure facilities. Between 1880 and 1914 some improvement occurred in all these areas and on the eve of the First World War the social role of beer in general and the public house in particular had begun to lose some of their importance. The social changes brought about by the First World War, however, greatly accelerated these pre-war trends. Heavy drinking became far less acceptable as a social habit; the younger generation spent much more of their time on a wide and growing range of leisure activities; housing conditions were greatly improved. As a result drunkenness ceased to be a major social problem as the traditional element of 'autonomous' consumption all but disappeared. The brewers were only too well aware that these fundamental changes in social attitudes and habits could not be reversed simply by reducing the price of beer. Social norms increasingly favoured moderate drinking, if not total abstention, and the brewers' only option was to seek to restore respectability to the public house. In these circumstances price competition was simply irrelevant.

The long-term contraction in the market, reinforced by restrictive licensing, affected competition in two other ways. Firstly, it meant that the only way in which a brewery company could increase its market share was to acquire additional tied outlets. From 1900 onwards this in effect compelled firms to expand by acquiring other firms. The extent to which firms actually competed in buying other firms and their properties, however, was limited by the behavioural standards of the industry, the strength of family ownership and control, and the market security conferred by the tied house system. Secondly, in so far as a falling level of consumption was symptomatic of a decline in the social importance of the public house, the trend could only be reversed if the brewers succeeded in making their houses far more attractive to the general public. In short the brewers began to compete with each other (and implicitly with suppliers of alternative goods and services in the leisure market) by providing better amenities in their houses. While the first tentative moves in this direction may be discerned in the decade before 1914, it was the market revolution of the inter-war period which generated effective competition in amenities. The first tangible results were seen in the 'improved' public houses which many firms, particularly the larger regional brewers, began to build during the 1920s. Although interrupted by the depression of 1929-33 and again by the Second World War and the succeeding period of 'austerity', the process of improving existing houses and building new ones gradually gained momentum. By the 1960s the policy of improvement was clearly achieving positive results in so far as the long drift away from public houses had been reversed. The public house was increasingly seen to be an important and effective competitor in the leisure market. The Monopolies Commission, while conceding that amenity standards had been greatly improved, still maintained that competition in the on-licensed trade focused on amenities because price competition was largely absent. In reality, however, the significance of competition in amenities can only be understood in the context of the social role of the public house and of its historical relationship with the problem of drunkenness.

The Commission also erred in arguing that because price competition existed in the take-home trade, measures designed to weaken the tie would automatically bring the same kind of rivalry into the on-licensed trade. The take-home trade in liquor is not essentially different from the retailing of any other type of product for mass consumption. Brand names and 'images' are certainly significant, but price rivalry is probably the main focus of competition in this sector. The on-licensed trade, however, is fundamentally different. The emergence of the national groups has affected the nature of competition in the on-trade by breaking down long-established local monopolies and introducing national brands into areas where they were not formerly available. To this extent it could be said that the range of consumer choice, at least in certain areas of the country, has been increased even though many local brands have disappeared. Yet the Monopolies Commission's emphasis on consumer choice in public houses once again betrays its failure to appreciate the peculiar nature of beer retailing. All the evidence we have gathered to date suggests that in practice only a small minority of drinkers are strongly influenced in their choice of public house by the range of beers available. The majority seem to attach more importance to the general character of the house itself, including the amenities, the clientele and the licensee. The public house is not — and in England and Wales never really has been — a mere drink shop, which customers visit with the same expectations as they would any other shop. It is therefore erroneous to apply to public houses the conventional yardsticks of competitiveness used in general retailing.

Social Responsibility and Economic Efficiency

The brewers' obligation to conduct their business in a socially responsible manner originally emerged as a response to those who argued that a 'dangerous trade' should either be suppressed altogether or transferred to public ownership. In practice, it was the threat of public ownership which proved to be by far the more significant of the two. The campaign for 'municipalisation' of the liquor trade gathered momentum during the 1870s and probably reached its peak during the First World War with the establishment of the State management scheme at Carlisle. The fact that it still carried some weight with the Royal Commission of 1929-31, despite the ambiguous results of State management, was partly due to the failure of successive governments from 1904 onwards to devise a comprehensive strategy for liquor licensing.

During the last quarter of the nineteenth cenury it was clear to most brewers, politicians and magistrates that the number of licensed houses was excessive. The conventional view assumed that there was a direct relationship between the number of retail outlets and the consumption of liquor. This assumption was repeatedly challenged on the grounds that drunkenness was an urban phenomenon, and in most cities and towns the ratio of licensed houses to population was far lower than in the relatively sober rural areas. The real problem was that the era of free licensing (1830-69) had also been, at least in its later stages, an era of rising consumption. The re-introduction of restrictive licensing prevented the number of on-licences from growing any further but it made no provision for licence reduction, and when beer consumption began to decline after 1876 such provision became essential. Until the number of licences was reduced, competition in the retail trade remained at a level which was in the interests of neither the brewer, nor the licensee, nor even the customer himself. The response of the State, however, was limited to the 1904 Act, and even this legislation was introduced only in reaction to the agressive policy adopted by several licensing benches in 1900-3 of closing houses on a large scale without compensation. The 1904 Act introduced an orderly framework for the reduction of licences with compensation, and over the next decade the most heavily-congested areas were cleared of redundant outlets. The principal weakness of the Act, however, lay in its limited objectives. It enabled brewers and magistrates to close down those houses which were either socially undesirable or commercially unprofitable or both, but it did nothing to encourage joint action to improve the remaining, 'non-redundant' houses. After 1904 the serious and widespread need for improvement was either ignored or actively frustrated by licensing justices who took the view that on no account must public houses be made more 'respectable' lest this should stimulate the demand for liquor. After the First World War attitudes began to soften and some brewers found that magistrates were less inclined to resist improvements solely on the grounds that these might encourage more drinking. Nevertheless, the immense backlog of work which still needed to be done tended to reinforce the position of those who advocated State ownership of the liquor trade.

The longer the Carlisle scheme was in operation the more questionable the rationale of public ownership became. Advocates of State management believed that the competitive 'pushing' of liquor in brewery-owned houses was responsible for excessive drinking. The tied tenant, it was argued, had an obvious interest in maximising his sales and this could never be in the interests of moderate drinking. A salaried civil servant, by contrast, would have no financial interest in the drink he sold and hence would ensure that the trade was conducted in a socially responsible manner. This argument, however, was based on a complete misunderstanding of the nature of the public house. A licensee, whether tied, free or paid by the State, did not 'push' the sale of drink but he certainly had to be responsive to the needs and preferences of his customers. The practical working of the Carlisle scheme effectively destroyed the old argument that a genuinely 'disinterested' system of public house management was either practicable or desirable. It also refuted the belief that State control of the liquor trade would result in a more rapid improvement of public houses than the brewers themselves could achieve. The record of State management in this field was certainly no better than that of comparable private firms, and probably fell short of the standards set by the most progressive brewers. Nor did the Carlisle scheme — despite its unfettered discretion to close redundant houses and breweries — achieve a better standard of performance in conventional economic terms than comparable private firms. The Carlisle scheme was supposed to show that under State ownership the liquor trade would be so conducted that both the social objective of promoting sobriety and the economic goal of using resources more efficiently would be achieved much more quickly than if the trade remained in private hands. Although the Royal Commission itself felt that the scheme had been successful and that State management should be extended, few other observers agreed.

The final collapse of the campaign for public ownership was attributable not only to the failure of the Carlisle scheme to live up to expectations, but also to the brewers' success in showing that private enterprise and social responsibility were not incompatible. When the Royal Commission of 1929-31 investigated this issue, the brewers were able to show that they had invested quite heavily in improving their houses without provoking a corresponding rise in the level of beer consumption. The success of the improvement programme, however, was limited by the continuing reluctance of many magistrates either to sanction improvements or to permit brewers to exchange new on-licences for old. It was also limited by the conservatism of many public house customers. It seems unlikely, therefore, that most improved houses were particularly profitable investments for the brewers, at least in the short term. In this sense, therefore, it could be said that profits were sacrificed in favour of social responsibility. If, however, the brewers had failed to adopt this strategy, they would obviously have played into the hands of those who argued that the trade would never be conducted in a responsible manner (in other words one conducive to increased sobriety) as long as it remained in private hands. The brewers also realised that in the prevailing climate of opinion their response to the declining level of demand must not be so aggressive as to leave them vulnerable to the accusation that they were deliberately seeking to encourage excessive drinking. The concept of social responsibility therefore enabled the brewers to rationalise their necessarily muted response to the market revolution.

Social responsibility was also a flexible doctrine and could be used to justify 'uncommercial' decisions: small, unprofitable public houses were kept open; breweries acquired through mergers were sometimes kept in operation for many years; brand names and product lines similarly acquired were often retained; large firms maintained friendly or 'gentlemanly' relations with their smaller neighbours. But while inefficient practices undoubtedly did exist, and some uncommercial decisions were made, the concept of social responsibility was by no means wholly to blame. The provisions of the 1904 Act, combined with the reluctance of magistrates to issue new licences, gave the brewers every incentive to preserve their 'colony of houses' intact, almost regardless of profit and loss criteria. The strength of family interests in the industry, reinforced by the entrenched conservatism of many drinkers, frequently justified the brewers' cautious approach to post-merger rationalisation. Relations with small firms were best conducted on a friendly basis partly because the tied house system gave the latter a degree of market security and partly because personal friendships were the *sine qua non* of mergers and acquisitions. The contracting market also exercised considerable influence over business policy. The emphasis in most firms was on maintaining the volume of output, which was seen almost exclusively in terms of supplying a traditional range of beers to a conservative clientele. The fact that the free trade was, up to the 1960s, a relatively small proportion of the market, and was in any case dominated by a few quasi-national firms, meant in practice that the output of most breweries had to be sold through tied outlets. These factors together help to explain firstly the lack of attention paid in most firms to marketing (as opposed to production), secondly the eagerness to expand through acquisition, and thirdly the reluctance to close public houses.

When, by contrast, the market began to expand and the framework of licensing became more flexible, the larger companies (and eventually the smaller firms) began to adopt a more 'commercial' approach to the management of their assets. The growth in the number of free trade outlets implied a corresponding diminution in the importance of tied trade, at least for the major firms. Horizontal concentration enabled the surviving firms to look at their tied outlets in a more pragmatic light. The need for heavy and sustained investment in public house amenities implied that resources must be concentrated on those properties which had growth potential and not spread thinly over an entire estate of good, bad and indifferent houses. The obvious need to raise the return on assets and, simultaneously, to induce tenants to compete more effectively in the leisure market produced radical changes in the traditional approach to the management of tenanted houses. Firms were no longer willing to invest large sums in public house improvement without taking steps to ensure that the investment would yield a reasonable return. Consequently the old 'wet rent' system was abandoned and tenants were given more incentive to respond like businessmen to a competitive market. These changes occurred even in firms where family influence was still pronounced, although it should be noted that the national groups began to recruit professional managers from other industries on a considerable scale.[3] The new approach to property management was complemented by an equally radical strategy in the field of product management. During the 1960s the growing importance of national brands, allied to the rapid growth of the free trade, enabled the larger firms to adopt a more aggressive approach to product rationalisation.

None of these far-reaching changes in business policy and practice could have occurred without a corresponding change in the brewers' approach to the concept of social responsibility. This does not, of course, mean that the brewers suddenly threw off all the traditional constraints on their business behaviour. Indeed, when the Erroll Committee (1972) took evidence on the question of dismantling the framework of restrictive licensing, the strongest advocate of 'no change' was the Brewers' Society. In the climate of the 1960s, however, the problem facing the brewers was how to maintain their social responsibilities without at the same time leaving themselves vulnerable to the accusation of seeking to preserve traditional restraints on competitive behaviour.

Thus the Brewers' Society told the Erroll Committee that in their view it would be dangerous to remove the justices' absolute discretion to grant new licences and renew existing ones:

> The number of public houses in any area would be regulated solely by ordinary market forces, and weaker establishments would, over a period of time, be forced out of business . . . the public interest would suffer during the deterioration of a failing pub because of the special problems created by the sale of alcohol for immediate consumption. The licensee would be tempted to engage in sales-pushing and would cut corners . . . In such a situation the 'atmosphere' of a pub is unlikely to be conducive to moderation.[4]

This argument would undoubtedly have been considered eminently responsible in the 1930s. To the members of the Erroll Committee, however, it sounded far too much like 'special pleading'. In their view:

> It also relies on the highly questionable assumption that the peculiar nature of the liquor trade justifies its insulation from all the ordinary processes of competition . . . If pressed to its logical conclusion, such an argument would deny the right to trade to anyone who could not prove that there was scope, in the locality, for his own premises as well as for those licensed outlets which are already operating. It is precisely this sort of situation which favours those already fortunate enough to possess licences at the expense of potential entrants to the trade . . . the argument . . . sounds too much like a defence of sectional and, to some extent, monopolistic interests.[5]

Here indeed was the crux of the problem. For decades the brewing industry had been officially regarded as a 'dangerous trade' in which the overriding criterion of conduct was 'responsibility' (i.e. restraint) rather than efficiency. From the early 1960s onwards the brewers made considerable efforts to bring their conduct and performance into line with the standards normally used in order to evaluate the efficiency of other industries. Nevertheless the continuing significance of vertical integration in the on-licensed trade attracted the unfriendly attention of those who applied the criteria of workable competition to the industry. In the 1920s, ultra-progressive brewers such as William Waters Butler and Sydney Nevile repeatedly justified their ownership of and managerial control over public houses in terms of the social benefits and safeguards which this brought to the trade and the public. In an age when drunkenness was still commonly related to the number and condition of public houses, 'responsible' management of these houses by the brewers was widely regarded as a fundamental necessity. By the late 1960s, however, public attitudes to drinking in general and the public house in particular had undergone a radical change. In the words of the Erroll Committee:

> For the vast majority of people alcohol is used not primarily as a drug from which to obtain some artificial stimulus, but as a social solvent, enjoyed as much for its taste as for its relaxing qualities, and that in the vast majority of cases it is incidental to some wider social purpose. . . . legislation ought not to be based on the assumption that it has to deal with a basically static social situation.[6]

The economic implications of this argument are self-evident. Once it is assumed that a major increase in the number of liquor-retailing outlets will not in general have undesirable social and moral consequences, restraints on competition — however justified they may have been in the past — can no longer be regarded as consistent with the public interest.

Licensing and Competition: The Implications of Change

To the extent that the social criteria for evaluating the conduct of the brewing industry have become increasingly blurred with, or subordinate to, conventional economic yardsticks, it is difficult to draw a clear distinction between them in discussing the case for changing the licensing system along the lines advocated by both the Monopolies Commission and the Erroll Committee. Nevertheless, an attempt will be made to distinguish between the economic case for change advanced by the Monopolies Commission and the broader, social reasons emphasised by Erroll.

Proceeding from the erroneous assumption that the tied house system was largely protected against competition by restrictive licensing, the Commission proposed that 'the licensing system in England and Wales should be substantially relaxed, the general objective being to permit the sale of alcoholic drinks, for on or off consumption, by any retailer whose character and premises satisfy certain minimum standards'.[7] The principal economic benefit which the Commission thought would arise from this relaxation was that the free trade would 'grow in size and strength at the expense of the tied trade'. As a result, there would be more wholesale price competition between brewers, the elimination of inefficient production capacity would proceed more quickly, new entrants would find it possible to break into the trade, the role of independent suppliers would be enhanced and the security of the tied house diminished. In evaluating this proposal, one could reasonably argue that the Commission greatly exaggerated the effect of restrictive licensing, if only because of the subsequent expansion of the free trade within the existing framework of law. Most of the economic benefits outlined above have in fact been realised since 1969 without any changes in the licensing system. As noted before, the Commission investigated the industry at a time when the national groups had barely begun to rationalise their assets and when the effects on the retail trade of increasing competition within the leisure market had hardly begun to emerge. But the Commission made a fundamental error in assuming that the free trade would grow at the expense of the tied trade. As argued previously, the take-home trade and the on-licensed trade offer complementary rather than competitive 'packages'. The take-home trade in alcoholic drinks is subject to the same price competitive pressures as any other form of high-street retailing; the on-licensed trade, however, offers a quite distinct package of amenities which, in total, reflect the social role of the public house.

The Commission wrongly assumed that price competition had been squeezed out of the on-licensed trade by vertical integration and concluded, therefore, that competition in amenities was strong *because* price rivalry was weak. In reality, however, the chain of causation works in the opposite direction. The social role of the public house means that competition must of necessity be focused on amenities, which in turn emphasises the importance of price flexibility rather than conventional price competition. It is of course true that the number of public houses has continued to decline in recent years and that for most breweries the relative importance of tied trade has diminished. But this does not necessarily mean that public houses have been driven out of business by competition from the free trade. It must be emphasised that since the 1960s the continuing reduction in the total stock of public houses has been due partly to the rationalisation programmes carried out by the national groups and partly to the continuing effects of urban redevelopment. To the extent that houses have been closed on economic grounds, the brewers have been able to concentrate their resources on improving those houses which they consider have a commercial future. It should also be remembered that in England and Wales over the period 1962-71 between 500 and 600 new full on-licenses (mainly public houses) were granted every year, with a tendency for the number to increase in the early 1970s.[8] The Erroll Committee's own evidence suggests that considerably more people were visiting public houses on a regular basis in the early 1970s than for many years. It can hardly be argued, therefore, that the public house is a declining institution and that the take-home trade has been growing at the expense of the on-licensed sector.

Can a major relaxation of the licensing system be justified on broader social grounds? The logic of restricting both the number of licensed houses and their hours of sale has always been based on an assumed relationship between the actual consumption of drink and opportunities which exist for its consumption. The evidence presented in this study, however, suggests that the relationship — if it exists at all — is much more complex than has been conventionally assumed. Indeed, it may be argued that as a deterrent to excessive drinking restrictive licensing can only be effective if it accords with the prevailing norms and expectations of society as a whole. Considered in this light, the gradual elimination of the problem of excessive drinking between 1914 and 1939 can be seen not as a victory for restrictive licensing but rather as the direct result of a series of fundamental changes in the quality of urban life. In this sense it could be said that restrictive licensing simply reflected the declining social importance of drink in general and the public house in particular. By the same token, the partial liberalisation of the licensing system in 1961, followed by Erroll's proposals for much more radical change, reflect the needs and aspirations of an era in which the role of drink as a 'social solvent' is increasingly regarded with approval. In these circumstances it would be surprising indeed if some of the restrictions inherited from the past were not looked upon as irksome. The evidence submitted to Erroll, for example, suggests that there is a significant demand for drinking in public to be made '. . . less of a family-dividing occasion' than it has traditionally been. Given the general reluctance to allow children under 16 years of age into public houses and bars, this demand may be satisfied only through 'a totally different concept of a place where the whole family could obtain refreshment'.[9] There also appears to be a demand that opening hours should be much more flexible and that licensees should be allowed to open and close their premises more in accordance with the ebb and flow of custom. The Erroll Committee recognised the legitimacy of this demand and made reasonable proposals for meeting it.[10]

The most significant restriction inherited from the past, however, is the absolute discretion of local justices to grant new licences and renew existing ones. The Erroll Committee advocated the limitation of this direction to certain specified criteria, which did not include that of the 'need' for a particular licence in a given locality:

The application of the test of 'need' to new applications for on-licences is out of date and unnecessary . . . the only relevant commercial consideration is that of market demand. A licensing authority is hardly qualified to assess whether such a demand exists, and we see no reason why any licensing process should interfere with the ordinary operation of market forces.[11]

The fact that over the period 1967-71 only about 8 per cent of the total number of applications for new public house licences were refused on the 'lack of need' criterion suggests that the practical effects of abolishing it would not be particularly significant. Nevertheless, the Erroll Committee was concerned to ensure that new sources of enterprise would be attracted into the retail liquor trade and argued that a significant number of potential licence applications may have been discouraged 'because the applicants knew that particular licensing benches had adopted a restrictive approach to the test of 'need''.[12] In fact the Erroll Committee endorsed the Monopolies Commission's view that the justices' traditional control over licensing had effectively concentrated public drinking in houses which were primarily designed for no other purpose. Anticipating a continued growth in the demand for a variety of leisure services, Erroll argued that the liquor trade should be allowed much more freedom to respond to market forces:

> We favour the greatest possible scope for flexibility and experimentation in the licensed trade. We see a need for more varied forms of catering at which drink can be served in the context of entertainment, family refreshment or in premises offering a variety of amenities. We think that the public should be given an opportunity of demanding, and of obtaining, facilities for drinking other than those offered by the public house and at different times from those permitted at present.[13]

In so far as these sentiments point to the likelihood that more flexibility in the on-licensed trade will be needed as leisure tastes become even more sophisticated, it is difficult to fault them.

Although there seems little prospect of the Erroll recommendations, or some variant upon them, being implemented for several years, it would not be out of place to speculate briefly on their implications for the market structure and conduct of the brewing industry. Firstly, would the flow of new entrants be significantly greater under a relaxed licensing system than it is at present? It is worth noting that the Erroll Committee itself was by no means certain that it would: 'We do not believe that there are, waiting in the wings, large numbers of prospective licensees, with sufficient capital, who are simply waiting for the relaxation of the 'need' criterion in order to build new public houses or convert existing buildings to that use.'[14] For the small entrepreneur the capital costs of entry into the free retail trade are high and, while the flow of new entrants has certainly increased since the 1960s, it would be naive to assume that the easier availability of licences will in itself have much effect on this flow. In practice, the Erroll strategy would probably encourage both the brewers and the large leisure groups to experiment on a limited scale with new types of outlet either directly or by means of loan facilities to private entrepreneurs. Secondly, would the brewers' control over the on-licensed trade in general be weakened and competition thereby enhanced? Again, it seems unlikely that there would be any dramatic changes. To the extent that small entrepreneurs moved into liquor retailing they might well find themselves in a position similar to that of many registered clubs. The rationale of the Erroll strategy (as distinct from that of the Monopolies Commission) is that freer licensing would encourage competition in the provision of different packages of amenities and would not necessarily result in a greater degree of price rivalry. This being so, it seems likely that in practice many of these entrepreneurs would be obliged to seek loan facilities from the brewers and the large leisure groups in order to provide the kind of amenities for which there was a demand. Since it must be assumed, realistically, that freer licensing would not in itself encourage new entry into the production of beer, these loan facilities would almost certainly be granted in return for some kind of tie on supplies, as has long happened in the club sector. While the loan-tie is obviously vulnerable to competitive pressures and, indeed, is frequently associated with wholesale discount rivalry between brewers, the net effect would be to keep the control of beer supplies firmly in the hands of the existing suppliers.[15]

This conclusion simply reinforces the point made earlier, namely that, in practice, it is easy to confuse the effects of vertical integration with those of horizontal market power. The Erroll strategy would not break down the oligopolistic structure of the brewing industry nor would it challenge the observed tendency for oligopolists to compete through the marketing mix rather than indulge in unrestrained price rivalry. Indeed, the Erroll Committee implicitly accepted that the existing level of horizontal concentration would continue, and drew a clear distinction '. . . between measures designed to remove those obstacles in the way of commercial development which are no longer justified on social grounds, and positive measures designed principally to manipulate the structure of the brewing industry in order to produce a specific effect'.[16] In practice, the Erroll recommendations would at most only accelerate the trends which have been gathering momentum within the brewing industry since the early 1960s, principally the development of a more varied package of amenities in the on-licensed trade and the growth of more outlets catering for the take-home trade within a framework of concentrated horizontal market power. The Committee emphasised that it had no intention of trying to weaken or in any way detract from the main benefit of vertical integration to the consumer, namely the improvement of amenities in public houses. In its evidence to the Monopolies Commission, the Consumer Council argued that public houses were '. . . not meeting the demand for something, though exactly what that something is remains a matter for dispute'. The Brewers Society, by contrast, maintained that there could be no presumption that '. . . all public houses should necessarily set out to feed and entertain the general public otherwise than by the supply of liquor in congenial surroundings'.[17] The chief merit of the Erroll strategy is that it would enable both the brewers and private entrepreneurs to estimate more accurately the significance of the demand for a 'non-traditional' package of amenities in the on-licensed trade and the extent to which that demand was not being met. The likelihood that it would have any additional effects on conduct and performance must remain problematical.

Oligopolistic Competition and the Public Interest

Does the foregoing analysis throw any light on the general nature of oligopolistic competition? Before this question can be answered, we must clarify the term oligopoly. It is now widely accepted that all that is required to produce oligopoly is not a particular number of firms in an industry, but simply that firms have to take account of the reactions of their rivals to their policy decisions. Such interdependence is 'virtually all-pervasive'.[18] It should not be assumed, therefore, that in the case of the brewing industry the relatively recent increase in horizontal concentration has produced an oligopoly where none previously existed. In this industry oligopoly first appeared in the London trade during the eighteenth century when large-scale production methods were widely adopted. The remainder of the industry became oligopolistic in the course of the nineteenth century as commercial brewing replaced publican brewing. Since then it has been impossible for any firm to take decisions on pricing, quality, product innovation, property acquisition and improvement and expansion through merger without considering the reactions of its rivals to those decisions. Yet despite, or perhaps because of, the prevalence of oligopolistic market structures, no comprehensive theory of oligopoly has yet been developed. Oligopolistic competition takes a multitude of different forms, the only characteristic common to all of them being that interdependence is assumed in

making competitive moves.

One approach assumes that oligopolists will normally attempt to monopolise the market jointly, either by tacit agreement on a collusive scheme of control or by simple recognition of their mutual inter-dependence. It then analyses the various uncertainties and difficulties of policy coordination which will systematically limit the oligopolists' joint profits.[19] The key point in this approach is that oligopolists will always seek to establish a competitive equilibrium and will often succeed in doing so. In his analysis of the brewing industry in the 1950s, Vaizey concluded that there was a 'natural oligopolistic equilibrium' which made formal collusion unnecessary. Two factors were said to be respon-sible for this situation. Firstly, the industry was wholly protected (by the tied house system and restrictive licensing) from outside competi-tion. Secondly, it was virtually impossible for 'rogue' firms to upset the equilibrium, at least in the short-run:

> The parties in the battle of the national brewers are too equal in size to go in for wars to the death (leaving aside the social conven-tions which make such a process unlikely), the local firms whose concessions to the bigger brewers represent victories in this war are too secure in their markets to be easily persuaded to yield much (without selling out at a very high price) and the free market is not sufficiently extensive to allow for more than tactical vic-tories or extensive field operations with no great triumphs. If the tied house system were to be abolished, this comfortable situation would cease to exist . . . a break of the tie would lead to an in-tensification of price agreements and possibly an increase in re-tailing and wholesaling selling activity.[20]

In short, the root cause of this competitive equilibrium was assumed to be vertical integration. The tied house system had, in effect, distributed market power so evenly throughout the industry that an oligopolistic stalemate had emerged.

This analysis clearly needs to be modified in the light of subsequent developments. The growth of a leisure market has tended to blur the demarcation lines which once separated the retailing of beer from other activities, while the expansion of the free trade has provided more scope for price competition. Moreover, during the 1960s many small firms found that the tied house system gave them inadequate protection against competitive trends in the demand for beer. These trends simply reinforce the conclusion advanced earlier in this study, namely that market power — the ability to determine supply terms without com-petitive encroachment — derives essentially from a firm's position of *horizontal* dominance of some market level and not from *vertical* integration as such. When Vaizey analysed the industry, the importance of small, local firms depended not only on the tied house system but also on the traditional strength of local tastes and preferences. If one looks at the industry's market structure from a purely national perspective, then the degree of horizontal concentration was undoubtedly low. If, however, one recognises the importance of product differentiation and local tastes, than the market structure must be viewed from a local or regional perspective. Most local markets were dominated by a relatively small number of firms, each of which, while having little influence outside their market, enjoyed a considerable degree of horizontal power within it. These firms did not begin to lose their market power until their staple product — cask beer — began to lose its share of the market to nationally-branded bottled and subsequently keg beers. The growth of a national market, and the corresponding decline in product differentiation, has in this sense helped to upset the competitive equilibrium described by Vaizey.

It would, therefore, be more accurate to say that since the 1960s the brewing industry has been characterised by oligopolistic *rivalry*. In the free trade this rivalry takes the form of competitive pricing, advertising and sales promotion. In the tied trade it takes the form of competition in providing better and more varied amenities. The growth of the national groups through acquisition has largely swept away the surviving elements of local monopoly. As the Monopolies Commission admitted, by the late 1960s the national brewers were competing directly with each other in almost every area of the country in both the free trade and the tied trade. The character of competition certainly differs between these two sectors, but the existence of rivalry is hardly in doubt. Indeed the widespread and unprecedented closure of tied houses by the national groups may be seen as symptomatic of the growth of competition in the on-licensed trade. Significantly, even some of the small independent firms are now adopting a more 'commercial' approach to the management of their tied estates.[21] Another important result of the growth of competition in the industry has been the achievement of greater 'dynamic' efficiency by the national groups. Old plant has been closed, new production facilities built and distribution systems rationalised in order to reduce unit costs. Product portfolios have also been rationalised and low volume lines eliminated. The elimination of small firms and the progressive integration of the national groups should also have promoted 'X-efficiency' and reduced organisational slack. While conclusive empirical evidence on this point is difficult to obtain, and the conventional financial ratios derived from balance sheet analysis should always be treated with caution, there is little support for the Price Commission's view that the national groups have failed to invest their resources efficiently. Finally, it has been pointed out that since oligopolistic competition is essentially a price-product mix it will, if effective, provide a favourable climate for innovation.[22] It must be conceded that from the 1880s through to the 1950s the industry witnessed little innovation in product development or in production techniques. The only major innovation was the development of chilled and carbonated bottled beer which, while of strategic long-term significance, spread only slowly through the industry. Since the 1950s, however, the rapid growth of keg beer, lager and canned beer suggests that the climate has become more favourable to innovation. If the Erroll Committee's strategy were to be implemented, it is likely that there would also be innovation, or at least more flexibility, in the package of amenities provided in the on-licensed trade.

Is the existing pattern of rivalry within the industry consistent with the conventional notions of workable competition? Stigler has suggested that 'an industry is workably competitive when, (i) there are a considerable number of firms selling closely related products in each important market area, (ii) these firms are not in collusion, and (iii) the long-run average cost curve for a new firm is not materially higher than that for an established firm'.[23] On these criteria the brewing industry would not be workably competitive. Do seven major producers constitute a 'considerable' number of firms? Does wholesale discount rivalry in the free trade offset the price leadership which the two or three biggest firms (Allied, Bass and Whitbread) seem to exert? The answer to both questions would appear to be negative. The third criterion obviously does not apply in the case of 'classic' entry, which was presumably what Stigler had in mind. It must be emphasised, however, that the inability of the industry to meet these critera is primarily a function of horizontal market power rather than of vertical integration. If public policymakers wish to make the industry conform to Stigler's idea of workable competition, they would not only have to prohibit brewery ownership of licensed outlets and outlaw the loan-tie but would also be compelled to reduce the existing degree of horizontal market power by dissolving the national groups. Leaving aside the immense practical problems involved in pursuing such drastic measures, critics of the industry must ask themselves whether, on balance, the public interest would be better served than under existing arrangements. As Vaizey has pointed out: '. . . in the absence of grave abuses it is difficult to argue persuasively against concrete advantages to compact groups'.[24] Successive investigations into the structure, conduct and performance of the brewing industry have conspicuously failed to reveal any such abuses. Indeed, it has been argued in the course of this study that in recent years, as these groups have become more 'compact' and their advantages more 'concrete', the general public in their role as consumers have derived certain tangible benefits.

The fundamental weakness in the approach of many exponents of workable competition is, of course, that they tend to exaggerate the significance of market structure as a determinant of conduct and performance. Consequently they see the effectiveness of competition in a given market primarily in terms of its structural characteristics. It has been argued in this study, however, that the existing market structure of the brewing industry is to some extent a reflexion of the way in which it has been conducted and has performed in the past. Thus vertical integration has been seen as an inherent feature of beer retailing in England and Wales long before the onset of restrictive licensing. Similarly, the rapid development of the tied house system in the late Victorian era reflected the extent to which the brewers had expanded their production capacity during the preceding period of market growth. This does not, of course, mean that vertical integration has in itself had *no* influence over the conduct and performance of the industry. But it must also be recognised that the traditional standards of conduct and performance were determined more by social and moral values than by economic criteria. Consequently the ownership of public houses by the brewers was both justified and attacked in terms of its relationship to the problem of excessive drinking. Changing social habits and the development of the improved public house enabled the brewers to argue convincingly that the tied house system, if conducted responsibly, was an indispensable element in the framework of social control. In practice, however, it proved difficult to reconcile social responsibility with the efficient use of resources, particularly in an era when the rigidities of the licensing law positively discouraged a flexible response to market trends. In this sense, the rapid horizontal concentration which occurred over the decade 1958-68 may be seen as a belated recognition of the need to improve on traditional standards of performance. Yet this recognition must also be seen against a background of changing social values.

Until relatively recently these values have tended to reflect the Victorian temperance reformer's view of the industry as a dangerous trade which, if it could not be abolished, must be closely controlled. Consequently brewers and licensees alike were expected to behave 'responsibly' and restrain their commercial instincts. Overt attempts by the brewers to stimulate liquor consumption would have left them vulnerable to the charge of seeking to increase drunkenness and would thus have played into the hands of those who argued that social responsibility could only be achieved through public ownership of the trade. The contemporary view, by contrast, tends to minimise the differences between the liquor trade and other manufacturing industries, and consequently regards with disfavour those restraints on competitive behaviour which have been inherited from the past. The Erroll Committee, for example, argued that 'what people are most concerned about when they discuss the tied house system is the fact that they are unable, in certain areas or in certain public houses, to obtain the drink they want because of the ownership of outlets by a particular brewery or breweries. In our view these are precisely the sort of consequences, whether one describes them as social or economic, which one would expect to be taken into account in considering whether a monopoly situation exists in any particular industry. Simply because the product happens to be beer is no reason for taking a different view than one would in the case of, for example, detergents, motor cars or any other consumer product'.[25] In short, the 'public interest' in the structure, conduct and performance of the brewing industry has been defined quite differently at different stages of the industry's development.

The perceived interaction between social and economic norms which has shaped the character of competitive behaviour in the brewing industry over the past century or more suggests that conventional notions of workable competition can, at best, provide only a one-dimensional perspective. In Markham's words:

> A possible alternative approach to the concept of workable competition . . . is one which shifts the emphasis from a set of specific structural characteristics to an appraisal of possible remedial action. A first approximation to the concept of workable competition when viewed along these lines might be as follows: an industry is workably competitive when, after its market characteristics and the dynamic forces which shaped them have been thoroughly examined, there is no clearly indicated change that can be effected through public policy measures which would result in greater social gains than social losses.[26]

The main difficulty with this broader approach is, of course, that in practice it might be used simply to justify the *status quo*. Nevertheless it seems particularly appropriate to the brewing industry, where business policy has a pronounced social and moral dimension. Judged in Markham's terms, the industry must be considered to be workably competitive. This does not necessarily mean that public policy should adopt a stance of benign neglect towards the industry. Competition policy still has a legitimate interest in ensuring that the current level of rivalry is maintained and if possible extended. In this context a persuasive case can be made for the implementation of the Erroll proposals, or something very similar, on the grounds that this would give the brewers even greater incentives to compete both with each other and with alternative suppliers of leisure services in the retail market. Beyond essentially marginal intervention of this kind, however, it is difficult to see how public policy could increase the level of competition in the industry without producing both losses to the consumer and wider social costs which would more than outweigh the benefits.

References and Notes

1 Introduction

1. J. E. Vaizey, *The Brewing Industry, 1886-1952*, Pitman 1960, p. 151.
2. A. Seldon, 'The British Brewing Industry', *Lloyds Bank Review*, October 1953.
3. Vaizey, op. cit., p. 156.
4. Seldon, op. cit.
5. J. M. Clark, 'Toward a Concept of Workable Competition', *American Economic Review*, June 1940.
6. The essential distinction is between the 'structural' approach, which involves a direct attack on the possession of market power, and the 'conduct' approach which is concerned exclusively with the way in which that power is exercised. Under the structural approach, the formation of 'unreasonable' concentrations of market power by mergers is restricted and such concentrations already in existence may be dissolved. The anti-trust laws in the USA reflect this structural approach. By contrast, the conduct approach (which has dominated public policy in the UK) is concerned with regulating the exercise of market power by individual enterprises, or groups of enterprises, where this is associated with some specific abuse or with relatively poor market performance.
7. Clark, op. cit.
8. Specifically, market theory predicts that in the long run firms in a purely competitive market secure only 'normal' profits. Buyers are charged a price equal to marginal cost, and this price is consistent with the lowest attainable cost of supplying the product. The possession of market power, by contrast, is shown to afford firms a degree of protection from the competitive forcing of prices towards marginal costs, enabling firms to enjoy 'excessive' profits. There is, in fact, some empirical support for the hypothesis that markets exhibiting higher seller concentration and restricted entry generate a significant degree of resource misallocation due to monopolistic pricing — see J. S. Bain, *Industrial Organisation*, Wiley 1968.
9. James W. McKie, *Tin Cans and Tin Plate*, Harvard University Press 1959, p. 7.
10. G. C. Allen, *Monopoly and Restrictive Practices*, Allen and Unwin 1968, p. 23.
11. J. M. Clark, *Competition as a Dynamic Process*, The Brookings Institution 1961, p. 472.
12. J. A. Schumpter, *Capitalism, Socialism and Democracy*, Allen and Unwin 1947, Chapters 7 and 8.
13. O. E. Williamson, 'Economics as an Anti-Trust Defence: The Welfare Trade-Offs', *American Economic Review*, 1968.
14. O. E. Williamson, *The Economics of Discretionary Behaviour: Managerial Objectives in a Theory of the Firm*, Mark Lane Publishing 1967.
15. H. Leibenstein, 'Allocative Efficiency vs X-Efficiency', *American Economic Review*, June 1966; see also Charles K. Rowley, *Antitrust and Economic Efficiency*, Macmillan 1973.
16. Clark, 1961, p. 481.
17. E. A. G. Robinson, *The Structure of Competitive Industry*, Cambridge University Press 1958, p. 110.
18. Monopolies Commission, Report on the Supply of Beer, HMSO, 1969.
19. F. Machlup and M. Taber, 'Bilateral Monopoly, Successive Monopoly and Vertical Integration', *Economica*, May 1960.
20. O. E. Williamson, 'The Vertical Integra-

tion of Production: Market Failure Considerations', *American Economic Review*, May 1971.

21. J. S. Bain, *Barriers to New Competition*, Harvard University Press 1956, p. 145.

22. Williamson (1971), op. cit.

23. R. H. Bork, 'Vertical Integration and the Sherman Act: the Legal History of an Economic Misconception'. It is worth noting that in its report on the supply of petrol (1965), the Monopolies Commission attributed the lack of retail price competition to the oligopolistic nature of the market rather than to vertical integration.

24. Bain, op. cit.

25. More specifically, these benefits include (i) allocative efficiency, whereby supply prices and quantities should be consistent (in the long run) with the real factor costs of supplying the product, (ii) technical efficiency, whereby production costs should be the 'lowest attainable' within the prevailing technology, (iii) distributive efficiency, whereby physical distribution costs should be consistent with the lowest attainable channel costs, (iv) technological progressiveness, whereby firms should actively seek to develop and introduce new products and production techniques.

26. Price Commission, Report No. 31, 'Beer Prices and Margins', HMSO 1977.

27. A. D. Chandler, *Strategy and Structure*, Massachusetts Institute of Technology 1962.

28. D. Swann, D. P. O'Brien, W. P. J. Maunder, W. S. Howe, *Competition in British Industry*, Allen and Unwin 1974, pp. 106-107.

29. Price Commission, op. cit.

30. John Vaizey, op. cit., p. 155.

2 Background to the Modern Industry

1. J. E. Vaizey, 'The Brewing Industry', in *Effects of Mergers*, P. L. Cook and R. Cohen, Allen and Unwin, 1958, pp. 399-400.

2. Ibid, p. 400.

3. B. R. Mitchell and P. Deane, *Abstracts of British Historical Statistics*, Cambridge University Press 1962, pp. 343-44.

4. S. G. Checkland, *The Rise of Industrial Society in England, 1815-1885*, Longman 1964, p. 233.

5. Monopolies Commission, Report on the Supply of Beer, HMSO, 1969, Appendix 8, pp. 153-58.

6. Ibid.

7. G. B. Wilson, *Alcohol and the Nation*, Nicholson and Watson 1940.

8. Ibid, p. 84.

9. As Mathias has pointed out, the loan tie gave the brewers the advantages of being creditors without the responsibility of being landlords; see P. Mathias, *The Brewing Industry in England, 1700-1830*, p. 133.

10. G. B. Wilson, op. cit.

11. P. Mathias, op. cit., pp. 15-25.

12. L. A. G. Strong, *A Brewers' Progress, 1757-1957*, London 1957.

13. P. Mathias, op. cit., p. 226.

14. *The Brewers' Almanack*, 1833.

15. Ibid, p. 155-6.

16. Bass Board Minute Books.

17. A. Barnard, *Noted Breweries of Great Britain*, Sir Joseph Causton and Sons 1889, Vol. I, pp. 301-27.

18. Ibid, p. 240.

19. In 1874, for example, the chairman of the Kirkstall Brewery Co. Ltd. told his shareholders that the directors proposed to 'withdraw the loans from London and put them as well as they could in the country'.

20. 'Looking at the matter from a general trade point of view, we cannot help feeling alarm at this rapid decline in the number of brewers, and fear that this gradual concentration of the trade may result in the development of huge monopolies. . . .' *The Brewers' Guardian*, 26 February 1884.

21. *The Brewers' Guardian*, 27 January 1885.

22. The Chairman of the Lion Brewery Co. Ltd., for example, in announcing that the company was to raise £120,000 stated that 'the reason why they wanted more money was for the maltings . . . in manufacturing their own malt they effected a very great saving. . . .' *The Brewers' Guardian*, 17 February 1880.

23. P. Mathias, op. cit., p. 254.

24. The ancillary trades such as malting and hop merchanting continued to supply new entrants to commercial brewing; William Tetley in Leeds (1872), James Eadie in Burton (1856) and Henry Mitchell in Smethwick (1866) all came from the ancillary trades.

25. P. Mathias, *The Brewing Industry in England, 1700-1830*, op. cit.

26. J. E. Vaizey, *The Brewing Industry, 1886-1952*, Pitman 1960, p. 400.

27. S. and B. Webb, *The History of Liquor Licensing in England*, London 1903, pp. 88-9.

28. D. M. Knox, 'The Development of the Tied House System in London', *Oxford Economic Papers*, Vol. 10, (New Series), 1958, pp. 66-83.

29. Select Committee of the House of Commons on Public Breweries, 1817.

30. L. Levi, *The Liquor Trade*, London 1871.

31. Monopolies Commission, Report on the Supply of Beer, op. cit., p. 155.

32. A. E. Dingle, 'Drink and Working Class Living Standards in Britain, 1870-1914', *Economic History Review*, 25, 4, 1972.

33. G. C. Allen, *British Industries and their Organisation*, Longman 1958.

34. Vaizey, op. cit., p. 403.

35. *The Brewers' Guardian*, 23 November 1880.

36. *The Brewers' Guardian*, 24 February 1874.

37. *Duncan's Brewery Manual*, 1889-94.

38. *The Financial News*, 2 March 1890.

39. Joshua Tetley and Son Ltd., *A Century of Progress*, Leeds 1923, p. 18.

40. *The Country Brewers' Gazette*, 28 June 1890.

41. Home Office Return, 1892.

42. Royal Commission on Licensing (1896-1899) Report, Chapter 10, p. 65.

43. *The Financial Times*, 9 December 1889.

44. *The Brewers' Guardian*, 3. July 1871.

45. *The Financial Times*, 8 August 1900.

46. D. M. Knox, op. cit.

47. Home Office Return, 1892.

48. D. M. Knox, op. cit.

49. There was no shortage of publicans prepared to sell their leases. The combination of high prices paid for leases by brewers and the insecurity of tenure engendered by the 1869 Act proved a sufficient inducement.

50. Vaizey, op. cit., pp. 404-5.

51. In 1914 nearly 80 per cent of British companies were still privately owned — see G. C. Allen, op. cit.

52. Vaizey, op. cit.

53. J. E. Vaizey, *The Brewing Industry*, op. cit. p. 405.

54. *The Country Brewers' Gazette*, 23 August 1888.

55. *The Brewers' Guardian*, 29 August 1893.

56. *The Brewers' Gazette*, 4 August 1910.

57. *The Country Brewers' Gazette*, 12 February 1903.

58. Monopolies Commission, op. cit., Appendix 8.

59. *The Brewers' Gazette*, 7 May 1908.

60. G. B. Wilson, op. cit., p. 381.

61. Vaizey, op. cit.

62. There is no doubt that the lack of licensing control over the growth of clubs challenged the logic of the prevailing strategy towards public houses. For what was the point of closing 'redundant' public houses or subjecting them to a system of rigorous control and supervision, when clubs could escape all these constraints?

63. *The Country Brewers' Gazette*, 2 January 1902.

64. *The Brewers' Gazette*, 9 November 1911.

65. G. B. Wilson, op. cit., p. 384.

66. M. A. Utton, 'Some Features of the Early Merger Movements in British Manufacturing Industry', *Business History*,

Vol. 14, January 1972.

67. *The Brewers' Gazette*, 3 July 1911.

68. *The Brewers' Gazette*, 16 July 1914.

69. G. B. Wilson, op. cit., pp. 432-33.

70. Royal Commission on Licensing (1929-31) Report, para. 456.

71. In 1914 expenditure on alcohol accounted for 8.5 per cent of total consumer spending; by 1938 this had declined to 6.5 per cent.

72. Monopolies Commission, op. cit.

73. W. W. Butler, Mitchell and Butler Ltd., Annual General Meeting, 1917 and 1918.

74. *The Brewing Trade Review*, 1 April 1930.

75. Royal Commission on Licensing (1929-1931) Report, p. 67.

76. Ibid. pp. 105-6.

77. Monopolies Commission, op. cit. After the war various associations of clubs got together to establish their own 'club breweries': for example, The Leeds and District Clubs' Brewery Ltd. (1919).

78. *The Brewing Trade Review*, 1 July 1926.

79. Royal Commission on Licensing (1929-1931), Minutes of Evidence.

80. One of the principal objectives of the Carlisle scheme was to show that public houses could be improved more quickly than under private enterprise. In the event this aim was not realised. The State Management Scheme's record of public house improvement was no better than that of many of the larger private concerns.

81. Ind Coope Annual General Meeting, 1933.

82. For much of the interwar period, the transport costs of most provincial brewers accounted for less than 4 per cent of the retail price of a barrel, and only exceeded 4 per cent when the radius of the delivery area rose above 30 miles.

83. H. Leak and A. Maizels, 'The Structure of British Industry', *Journal of the Royal Statistical Society*, No. 108, 1945, pp. 46-59.

84. Censuses of Production, 1930 and 1935.

85. For many of the smaller concerns although production costs are generally higher compared to the larger companies, this is offset by lower administrative charges and other overhead expenses, while transport and promotional costs are usually smaller per barrel/crate. *The Financial Times*, 17 April 1972.

86. L. Hannah, 'Takeover Bids in Britain Before 1950: An Exercise in Business 'Pre-History'', *Business History*, January 1974.

3   Developments in the Industry Since 1950

1. John Vaizey, *The Brewing Industry 1886-1952*, Pitman 1960, p. 68. In the early 1950s, cheap staple draught beer (produced mainly by local and regional brewers) accounted for 50 per cent of total production by volume, but only 36 per cent of sales by value.

2. Ibid., p. 60. Guinness supplied about 7 per cent of total beer consumption in the UK in the form of bottled stout. The other 'nationals' concentrated on a relatively small number of brands e.g. Ind Coope's *Double Diamond*, Whitbread's *Pale Ale* and *Mackeson's Stout*, Bass's *Blue Triangle* and Worthington's *Green Shield*.

3. *The Brewing Trade Review*, June 1954.

4. A. H. Halsey (Ed.), *Trends in British Society Since 1900*, Macmillan, 1972, p. 552. Simultaneously cinema-going began to lose its popularity. In 1946 cinema admission reached a peak of 1,635 million; by 1960 this had dropped by two thirds.

5. Traditional draught (or 'cask') beer was drawn up from the cellar to the bar by means of a beer machine operated by the barman. As the beer was drawn off, so air was admitted into the cask through a 'bung hole'. As the volume of air in the cask increased, so the carbon dioxide in the beer escaped so that eventually it

became 'flat'. The advent of air also encouraged bacteria and any particles of yeast to become active, so that the beer might assume a cloudy appearance and acquire an acidic taste. Once installed in the publican's cellar, cask beer had, on average, a life of only ten days before the processes outlined above began to take effect.

6. In 1972 the brand leader in the keg market was Allied Breweries' *Double Diamond* (with 25 per cent of total sales), followed by Bass Charrington's *Worthington E* (15 per cent), Whitbread's *Tankard* (15 per cent), Watney's *Red*, formerly *Red Barrel* (14 per cent), Scottish and Newcastle's *Younger's Tartan* (13 per cent) with the remainder of the market accounted for by several other quasi-national and regional brands – see *E.I.U. Retail Business*, No. 174, p. 23.

7. In 1976 the brand leader in the lager market was *Harp*, brewed by a consortium of Guinness, Scottish and Newcastle and Courage, with 21 per cent of the total market. In second place came Bass Charrington's *Carling* (21 per cent), followed by Allied's *Skol* (17 per cent), Whitbread's *Heineken* (14 per cent), Watney's *Carlsberg* (12 per cent) and Bass's *Tennent's* (8 per cent) – see *E.I.U. Retail Business*, No. 226, p. 30.

8. Price Commission, op. cit., p. 7.

9. Vaizey, op. cit., p. 76; Price Commission, op. cit., p. 4.

10. Vaizey, for example, observed that 'a regional firm intent on expansion will gradually shade its wholesale margin so that it captures the free trade in an area, and the local brewers then become entirely dependent on their tied trade'. Vaizey, op. cit., p. 72.

11. One former executive of Charrington & Co. Ltd., for example, told the present writers that 'prior to about 1954 the older directors didn't want to know about free trade – they felt that this was simply an area in which you made debts'. From the mid-1950s onwards, Charring-

ton began to push their bottled *Toby Ale* in the free trade, although even at its peak in 1959 this brand accounted for little more than 5 per cent of the company's total sales.

12. Monopolies Commission, op. cit., p. 68, para. 247; Evidence of Brewers' Society to Price Commission, 1977.

13. At constant 1970 prices, consumer spending on beer rose from £1.41 billion to £1,64 billion between 1971 and 1976; over the same period expenditure on wines and spirits rose from £1.03 billion to £1.59 billion – see *E.I.U. Retail Business*, No. 232, p. 12.

14. Sales of table wine doubled between 1970 and 1973. Nevertheless, the pattern of sales still reflected a strong regional bias towards London and the South East (33 per cent of total sales in 1972) and an even stronger social bias towards middle class consumers (social group AB accounted for 50 per cent of total consumption in 1972). Even in 1976 it was estimated that half the drinking population of the UK had never tasted table wine – see *E.I.U. Retail Business*, No. 225, pp. 42-3, and *Financial Times*, Survey of Beer Wines and Spirits, 28 June 1977.

15. Fielding, Newson-Smith & Co, 'Investment Analysis of the Brewery Industry', February, 1972

16. Nevertheless, one or two Whitbread directors (including the chairman himself) sat on the boards of most of their 'umbrella' companies and must in practice have exercised some influence over their general policies.

17. As Col. Whitbread explained at the 1956 A.G.M.: 'We continue to maintain the policy [of bottling our own beers] but in some cases where we have a financial interest in a company, we will contract them to bottle for us, provided this is carried out under the supervision of our own technicians on plant up to our own standards'.

18. One such arrangement was with Hammonds United Breweries Ltd. of Bradford

which by 1959 owned about 950 licensed houses, mainly in the West Riding. Although Ind Coope had no 'umbrella' holding in Hammond, the reciprocal arrangement was cemented by an exchange of directors. In return for selling *Double Diamond* through some of their outlets, Hammond sent draught beer to the relatively small number of houses owned by Ind Coope in the north. A similar arrangement was operated in respect of the Cornbrook Brewery Co. Ltd of Manchester. In other cases, Ind Coope adopted a more radical strategy in order to secure more outlets for *Double Diamond*. In 1959 Phipps Breweries Ltd (Northampton) bought 153 houses from Ind Coope for £650,000, and agreed that it would continue to sell certain of the latter's beers for 15 years thereafter provided that Ind Coope continued to take supplies of Guinness and mineral waters from the company. Of the 159 properties involved, 140 had originally belonged to the Brackley Brewery Co. (acquired by Ind Coope during the 1930s) and were all situated within a 45 mile radius of Phipps' Northampton base — see *The Brewing Trade Review*, September 1959.

19. This was in addition to the 18,000 free trade outlets which the group already supplied — see *The Investors' Chronicle*, 24 November 1961.

20. From 1956 onwards, however, a growing proportion of Watney's trade with these independent firms was in *Red Barrel*, the first national keg beer in the market.

21. Vaizey, op. cit., pp. 61-2. He estimated that the larger regional brewers accounted for about 35 per cent of total beer output and sales, or 40 per cent if their sales of national beers were taken into account.

22. Cameron's acquired John J. Hunt Ltd. of York in 1953 and the latter's subsidiary Scarborough and Whitby Breweries Ltd. Vaux's principal acquisitions were Lorimer and Clark Ltd. (1946), Steel Coulson & Co. Ltd. (1954) and Thomas Usher

& Son Ltd. (1959) — all of Edinburgh. and also Hepworth & Co. Ltd. of Ripon (1947).

23. The merger between Watney and Mann was prompted primarily by the former's decision to sell its Stag brewery (Pimlico) for redevelopment and to concentrate on developing its newer site at Mortlake. Mann's Whitechapel Brewery, however, was needed in order to bridge the gap in production capacity which would arise between the closure of the Stag brewery and the full development of Mortlake.

24. One major reason for the merger proposal was the heavy prospective cost of building new public houses in the Birmingham area. Mitchells and Butlers wished to avoid what they regarded as wasteful competition in securing and developing new sites. The merger failed to materialise primarily because the two boards could not agree upon who was to occupy the key positions in the merged organisation. In 1957, however, the idea of co-operation was partially realised when the two companies set up Associated Midland Breweries Ltd.

25. Hammonds acquired 12 small companies between 1946 and 1960, mainly in Yorkshire, although one small firm in East Lancashire and two in the Furness area were bought. Greenall Whitley consolidated their position in Lancashire and moved down into Cheshire and Shropshire, acquiring Magee Marshall of Bolton (1958), the Chester Northgate Brewery (1949) and the Shrewsbury and Wem Brewery (1951). J. W. Green acquired 8 companies between 1945 and 1956, situated predominantly in the midlands, the most important of which was Flower of Stratford (1954). Tennant Bros. extended their trade both north and south of Sheffield, purchasing Clarkson's Old Brewery, Barnsley (1956), the Nottingham Brewery (1944) and the Worksop and Retford Brewery (1959). Tetley moved into Lancashire (Cunningham of Warrington, 1951) and south

Yorkshire (Duncan Gilmour of Sheffield, 1954). Simonds of Reading, however, were one of the most ambitious firms, acquiring 5 firms in the post-war decade, stretching from Cornwall to Bristol.

26. Many regional and a few local firms acquired small wine and spirit merchants and soft drink manufacturers during the 1950s. The rate of growth in these markets relative to that of beer made this limited degree of diversification attractive to any brewery company in search of more profitable business. Wines, spirits and soft drinks together accounted for about 25 per cent of the gross profits in the retail trade during the 1950s.

27. Cohen and Cooke, op. cit., p. 420.

28. Brewery companies in this position, however, were seldom attractive as acquisitions, and only those firms who pursued a policy of expansion at almost any cost tended to enter the market for them. Hope and Anchor Breweries Ltd., a small Sheffield firm, was a particularly eager purchaser of smaller companies. This firm had concentrated on the production of bottled beer, namely *Jubilee Stout*, since the late 1930s and had sold other brewers' draught beers through its 200 tied houses in return for an undertaking on their part to sell *Jubilee* through their own houses. As a result, Hope and Anchor was under continued pressure to expand its tied estate. The firm's financial resources were such, however, that only limited and relatively cheap purchases could be made. It soon emerged that beer sales in most of the houses acquired by H. & A. were declining due to the 'very poor' condition of the latter — see H. & A. Board minute book.

29. When Charrington & Co. Ltd. acquired the Kemp Town Brewery in 1954, the idea of a merger between the two companies was nearly twenty years old. Charrington's chairman had an informal understanding with the chairman and major shareholder of the Kemp Town

Brewery that when the latter was ready to join a larger concern, he would give Charrington first option. On a smaller scale, in 1959 Hammonds acquired R. F. Case & Co. Ltd. of Barrow-in-Furness through similarly personal connexions.

30. The 1958 Census of Production reveals that out of 125 product groups, the concentration ratio in the brewing industry, measured by the share of net output attributable to the *three* largest firms, ranked only 93rd — see Nicholas Stacey, *Mergers in Modern Business,* Hutchinson 1966, pp. 125-7.

31. Douglas Kuehn, *Takeovers and the Theory of the Firm,* Macmillan 1975, pp. 16-19.

32. S. Aaronovitch and Malcolm Sawyer: *Big Business/ Theoretical and Empirical Aspects of Concentration and Mergers in the United Kingdom,* Macmillan 1975.

33. Whitbread & Co. Ltd., annual meeting, 1955.

34. *The Economist,* 30 May 1959; 12 September 1959.

35. Following Clore's opening bid of 60s., the price of Watney's ordinary shares rose quickly to 77s.

36. *The Observer,* 31 January 1965.

37. It was estimated that in 1958 the average book value of Ind Coope's 5000 properties stood at £6,400. Bass's fixed assets were similarly undervalued. In 1960 the apparent net asset value per share was 14s. 5d., but it was estimated that an up-to-date valuation would have lifted that figure above the current market price of 24s., (*Investors' Chronicle,* March 4th 1960). Similarly, the net asset value of Charrington & Co. Ltd. stood at 66s. 6d. a share in the 1960 balance sheet, whereas an up-to-date valuation would have raised that figure above the 100s. mark, the prevailing share price being 93s. 6d., — see *Investors' Chronicle,* 1 July 1960.

38. In 1959 Hammonds United Breweries acquired Westoe Breweries Ltd., a small family firm with a brewery and 90 houses in and around Durham. H.U.B. offered

52s. for each of Westoe's £1 ordinary shares, which was in fact 7s. a share less than the pre-bid market price. The older family directors, however, felt that they had given their word to H.U.B. and that it would have been ethically wrong for them to have invited a bid from another quarter.

39. This was in fact a reciprocal trading agreement whereby H. & A. sold *Carling* in the UK while Canadian Breweries sold *Jubilee Stout* in Canada. The Canadian sales of *Jubilee*, however, never approached break-even point, while H. & A.'s sales of *Carling* were little more than 100 barrels a week. Taylor was slow to grasp the significance of the tied house system, believing that other brewers would sell *Carling* simply because it was a fine lager.

40. Even so, the number of houses owned by Scottish brewery companies remained small by comparison with those held by English firms of similar size. One of the largest firms in the west of Scotland J. & R. Tennent of Glasgow (acquired by Charrington United Breweries in 1963) owned fewer than 200 houses before it added another 100 outlets to its tied estate with the purchase of Maclachlan & Co. Ltd. in 1960.

41. The Scottish brewers paid far higher prices for public houses than their English counterparts because in Scotland licensed premises were sold as independent businesses in their own right, involving substantial payments for goodwill. As late as 1967, only 27 per cent of licensed hotels and public houses in Scotland were owned by brewers.

42. The companies acquired were George Younger & Son Ltd., Alloa; John Fowler & Co. Ltd., Prestonpans; William Murray & Co. Ltd., Edinburgh; James Aitken & Co. Ltd., Falkirk; and James Calder & Co. Ltd., Alloa. In total they owned about 350 licensed houses and were responsible for about 20 per cent of aggregate beer output in Scotland. Nevertheless, they also brought overdrafts totalling

£1 million into United Breweries, together with a good deal of worn-out production plant.

43. Bass responded to Hancock's approach by taking 25 per cent of the latter's equity. In the event, however, Hancock were formally acquired by Bass Charrington in 1968 as a 'tidying up' operation which greatly strengthened the group's interests in South Wales.

44. Taylor's first offer for Bristol Georges was made direct to the shareholders against the opposition of the board. Courage responded with a higher offer and began buying the company's equity on the market. By the time Taylor increased his offer, Courage had already gained sufficient acceptances to give them majority control.

45. *The Times,* 30 March 1961. There were, of course, one or two other reasons for the merger. The defection of Hammonds to the rival United Breweries group had left a large gap in Ind Coope's reciprocal trading coverage in Yorkshire, which Tetley could more than fill. Ansell for their part had no further opportunities to expand by acquiring small firms in the Midlands for the simple reason that all the obtainable ones had already disappeared. Consequently Ansell were compelled to look further afield.

Having achived national coverage, Ind Coope, Tetley and Ansell (Allied Breweries) was not particularly active as regards further acquisitions, relying instead on a more intensive product-promotion strategy to sustain the growth of the group. Additionally, Allied felt that a strong range of nationally available and advertised brands was essential in order to secure representation in the growing free trade sector.

There were some take-overs, however. In 1963 Allied acquired the Guildford-based Friary Meux brewing concern, while in 1968 it expanded its wine interests by acquiring Showerings Vine Products and Whiteways. Its later efforts to expand its overseas brewing interests through a merger with Unilever and the further development of its hotel interests through a merger with Trust House Fortes, though, proved abortive.

46. *The Sunday Times*, 19 June 1960.
47. *Investors' Chronicle*, 10 February 1961.
48. *The Financial Times*, 2 June 1961.
49. *The Yorkshire Post*, 28 May 1960.
50. The chairman of United Breweries, explained the groups's approach at the 1961 A.G.M.: 'The framework of our management organisation is planned on the basis of regional marketing of those products for which a substantial goodwill has long been established by our subsidiaries. Those products will remain the bulk of our business for a long time; at the same time they and tied outlets are the springboard from which we shall develop our national brands'.
51. During the 1950s the demand for Bass's traditional beers declined and the board was compelled to reduce the gravity of these beers in order to maintain profit margins. Bass's brand image in the market was increasingly old-fashioned, being associated (not inaccurately) with heavy-drinking manual workers. Worthington beers, however, had always had a less bitter, more bland flavour than those of Bass and during the 1950s sales of Worthington showed a steady upward trend. In reality, Bass's much vaunted expertise in the free trade was non-existent. Their idea of free trade was simply the traditional wholesale business with other brewers and independent bottlers; it did not encompass the notion of competing with other brewers for new business in free trade outlets. In terms of tied trade, Bass had always relied on large-volume houses in the heavy industrial areas and seaports, many of which were under direct management. During the 1950s, however, a growing number of these houses were closed under urban redevelopment programmes, forcing Bass to spend heavily on building new houses merely in order to retain its existing trade in these areas.
52. Bass's holding in Wilson and Walker amounted to about 20 per cent of the equity and dated back to the 1920s; one of the Bass directors had also sat on the Wilson board for many years. Bass's refusal to contest Watney's bid was particularly surprising in view of the fact that most of its trade in the Manchester area was conducted through Wilson and Walker.
53. Butler found itself in the same position as many other middle-sized brewery companies. The Butler family had only a small share of the equity and thus had no way of defending the company against an unwelcome take-over bid. Nor was there any scope for further growth through acquisition, for the simple reason that with the disappearance of Atkinson practically all the small companies in the West Midlands had already been absorbed by larger competitors. Thus, when M. & B. acquired Atkinson, the market price of Butler's equity rose sharply (in anticipation of a bid from M. & B.) and the board took the opportunity to sell out on favourable terms.
54. John Mark, 'The British Brewing Industry', *Lloyds Bank Review*, April 1974.

4 Market Structure and Competition

1. Price Commission, Report No. 31, 'Beer Prices and Margins', HMSO, 1977, pp. 44-5.
2. Monopolies Commission, 'Report on the Supply of Beer', HMSO, 1969, p. 113, para. 393.
3. Ibid., p. 115, para. 401
4. Ibid., p. 103, para. 359-360.
5. Ibid., p. 102, para. 355.
6. Ibid., p. 106, para. 371.
7. Ibid., pp. 98-9, para. 346.
8. Arthur Seldon, 'The British Brewing In-

dustry', *Lloyds Bank Review*, October 1953; see also *Brewing Trade Review*, February 1955.

9. N.B.P.I., Report No. 136, 'Beer Prices', Cmnd. 4227; Monopolies Commission, op. cit., HMSO, pp. 4-5, para. 17.

10. Price Commission, op. cit., p. 23, para. 3.14.

11. Truman had acquired a new management team early in 1970, which had closed down the firm's Burton brewery and exhanged its thin scatter of 73 public houses in the Midlands and the North for 36 Courage houses in the London area. Work had also begun on a new brewery next to the company's old plant in east London. A 'crash' public house modernisation programme was also initiated.

12. Grand Metropolitan was also interested in Watney's breweries in Belgium and its wine and spirit subsidiary, International Distillers and Vintners.

13. Imperial Tobacco, the dominant firm in the cigarette industry, had begun to diversify its interests in the mid-1960s in response to the slow growth of cigarette sales, mainly into the food industry with Golden Wonder Crisps (1965), H.P. Sauce (1967), Ross Group (1969) and Allied Farm Foods (1970). In 1972 it acquired Courage, Barclay and Simond. Two years before Courage had obtained a substantial number of new houses in the North with the acquisition of John Smith's Tadcaster Brewery. The fact the Courage board supported the Imperial bid came as a surprise to many in the industry who had expected Courage to merge eventually with Scottish and Newcastle in view of their complementary trading coverage. It appears, however, that Courage, like Watney, was thinking of expanding in the Common Market and felt that with the financial backing of IMPs this could be more effectively achieved.

14. Report of the Departmental Committee on Liquor Licensing, Cmnd. 5154 HMSO, 1972, p. 53. The survey found that 39 per cent of professional workers were regular beer drinkers, compared with 36 per cent of skilled manual workers and 42 per cent of unskilled manual workers.

15. Economist Intelligence Unit, *Retail Business*, No. 226, December 1976; No. 174, August 1972; No. 192, February 1974.

16. Report of the Departmental Committee on Liquor Licensing, p. 59, para. 5.06.

17. *The Financial Times*, 24 April 1974.

18. Monopolies Commission, op. cit., p. 103.

19. Ibid., p. 14, para. 45.

20. Vaizey, op. cit., p. 69.

21. The Price Commission reported that in 1974-76, 20 per cent of the small brewers' beer sales were composed of 'foreign' beer, compared with just over 10 per cent for the regional brewers and 11 per cent for the large firms (op. cit., pp. 10-12).

22. In 1974-76 both the small brewers and the regional firms sold less than one third of their output to the free trade — see Price Commission, op. cit., p. 8.

23. Bass Charrington's free trade loans, for example, rose from £9.1 million in 1967 to £14.6 million in 1972, and the company's sales to the free trade increased by an average of 8 per cent a year over the same period — company balance sheets.

24. Monopolies Commission op. cit., p. 111.

25. Monopolies Commission, op. cit., pp. 110-11, para 385.

26. Ibid., p. 79, para. 283.

27. Ibid., p. 18, para. 58.

28. Ibid., p. 98. para 344.

29. Ibid., p. 111, para. 386.

30 Kevin Hawkins, 'Brewer-Licensee Relations: A Case Study in the Growth of Collective Bargaining and White Collar Militancy', *Industrial Relations Journal*, 3, 1, Spring 1972.

31. Watney Mann's decision in 1970 to transfer 80 tenanted houses in the London area to management attracted a good deal of unfavourable publicity from which all the major brewers tended to suffer. But

Watney's were in a particularly difficult position, with only 15 per cent of their 6,550 houses under management (1968) and a low overall rate of return on capital. By contrast, nearly 75 per cent of Scottish and Newcastle's 1,900 houses, 36 per cent of Allied's 8,300 houses, and 37 per cent of Bass Charrington's 9,000 houses were all managed. Nevertheless the other major groups with large tied trade interests in the South — Courage and Whitbread — had relatively few houses under management.

32. In respect of draught beer (including lager) the Commission found that free houses consistently charged between 1p and 3p per pint more than the average price in tenanted and managed houses. Gross percentage margins favoured free houses by about 5 per cent on average. The Commission also found, however, (as the N.B.P.I. had done in the 1960s) that average retail prices in London and the South East were between 2p and 4p per pint higher than in the rest of England and Wales. The Commission offered no explanation for this regional differential, although presumably the higher overheads carried by retail outlets in this area (e.g. rent and rates) is an im-portant factor — see Price Commission, op. cit., pp. 27-8.

33. Ibid., p. 27, para. 4.4.

34. Net profit margins for the large brewers as a percentage of beer sales (including duty) were 10.8 per cent in 1974-76, compared with 15.5 per cent for the regional brewers and 17.7 per cent for the smaller brewers — see Price Commission, op. cit., p. 13.

35. Price Commission, op. cit., p. 35, para. 4.21.

36. N.B.P.I., Report No. 13, 'Beer Prices', HMSO, 1966, para. 9.

37. Brewers' Society, Reply to Price Commission Report, para. 6.6.

38. Price Commission, op. cit., p. 34, para. 4.16.

39. The rapid development of UK lager production has, of course, prevented foreign importers from maintaining their market share at its 1960 level. Had the British brewers not invested heavily in lager production they would no doubt have been accused of inefficiency, conservatism, insularity etc. But since they have succeeded in largely pushing foreign lagers out of the market, they have now laid themselves open to the charge of being 'monopolists'.

5 Performance And Efficiency

1. Monopolies Commission, Report on the Supply of Beer, HMSO, 1969. pp. 105-106, para. 368.

2. Vaizey, *The Brewing Industry, 1886-1952*, Pitman 1960, pp. 85.

3. The only exception to this general rule arises in respect of the 'waste' in a brewery. The Customs and Excise department assumes that a standard percentage of the volume produced by every brewery is wasted in some way or another and does not charge duty on it. In new breweries, however, wastage can be reduced to 2 per cent of total output. In a 2.5 million barrel plant such as the Bass brewery at Runcorn, each 1 per cent reduction in beer wastage would probably bring in savings of about £600,000, — see *The Financial Times*, 'Special Survey on Brewing', 24 April 1974.

4. Bass Charrington, for example, has retained two relatively small breweries in Sheffield (formerly belonging to Hope and Anchor Breweries Ltd. and William Stones & Co. Ltd.), one in Wolverhampton (formerly W. Butler & Co. Ltd.), and one in Walsall (The Walsall-Highgate Brewery Ltd.) principally because all these plants have traditionally produced beers which have been extremely popular within their respective localities and which would, if closed, provoke a strong

consumer reaction which might easily outweigh any technical economies derived from closure.

5. C. F. Pratten, *Economies of Scale in Manufacturing Industry*, University of Cambridge, Dept. of Applied Economics, Occasional Papers No. 28, 1971, pp. 72-6.

6. The brewing sector working party at N.E.D.O. anticipates that this planned growth of productive capacity will be 'more than adequate' to meet expected demand. Much of the expansion will concentrate on lager production, which may well acount for one third of total beer output in the UK by 1980, — see *The Financial Times,* Survey on Beer, Wines and Spirits, 2 June, 1977.

7. Net output per head in the brewing and malting industries rose from £1,250 in 1952 to £4,950 in 1970, reaching £6,600 in 1973 — see E. G. Wood, *Comparative Performance of British Industries,* Graham & Trotman 1975.

8. Vaizey, op. cit., p. 80.

9. Monopolies Commission, op. cit., p. 113, para. 393.

10. N.B.P.I., Report No. 136, 'Beer Prices', HMSO, 1969, p. 30.

11. Monopolies Commission, op. cit., p. 106, para. 370.

12. Monopolies Commission, 'Patrol' Report, HMSO, 1965.

13. Mr R. A. McNeile, Managing Director of Guinness, Statement at a Press Conference following the publication of the Monopolies Commission report. Quoted in the *Brewing Trade Review*, May 1969.

14. N.B.P.I., Report No. 13, 'Costs, Prices and Profits in the Brewing Industry', HMSO, 1966, p. 9.

15. Price Commission, op. cit., p. 17, para. 3.1.

16. It should also be remembered that different accounting conventions have important implications for the measurement of rates of return. Two companies, having identical activities and transactions, will disclose different accounting rates of return if, for example, one uses the straight-line method of depreciation whereas another uses the fixed percentage of 'reducing balance' method, or if they use different methods of valuing stocks. Similarly, two companies, earning identical discounted cash flow rates of return will disclose different accounting rates of return if their investments involve development or sales promotion — items which yield benefits over several years but are conventionally deducted from profits when expenditure is incurred. The normal accounting treatment of such expenditure represents, in effect, an extreme form of accelerated depreciation.

17. In its Report on Flour and Bread (1977), the Monopolies Commission accepted that it was justifiable in the circumstances to consider the profits on milling and baking combined and not to look at the result of those activities separately.

18. Price Commission, op. cit., p. 23, para. 3.10. To be fair to the Commission, the N.B.P.I. also made the same point: 'a large part of the cost of investments in tied houses is in practice borne by wholesale prices' — see N.B.P.I. Report No. 136, p. 13, para. 40. While not unjustified, this statement is consistent with the brewers' argument that such investment is justified by the integral role of tied houses in the production and sale of beer.

19. Price Commission, op. cit., p. 17, para. 3.1. The Commission had obviously seized on a statement made, but not developed, by the Monopolies Commission to the effect that the brewers' method of valuing their tied estates meant that 'the overall return on capital employed, *to some extent,* is predetermined' — see ibid., pp. 173-4.

20. Arthur Seldon, 'The British Brewing Industry', *Lloyds Bank Review,* October 1953.

21. *The Brewing Trade Review,* April 1958,

22. *Investor.s Chronicle,* 24 November 1961.

23. Conversely, some firms who traditionally had relied heavily on direct management

(e.g. Mitchell and Butler) began to transfer some of their smaller managed houses to tenancy. This naturally tended to offset transfers in the opposite direction, so that the proportion of brewers' on-licenses under management increased only slightly, from 23.6 per cent to 26.5 per cent, in 1967-73 — see 'Two Good Ways to Run the British Pub.', The Brewers' Society, 1973, p. 2.

24. See, for example G. D. Newbould, *Management and Merger Activity*, Guthstead 1970; A. Singh, *Take-Overs*, University of Cambridge, Dept. of Applied Economics, Monographs, No. 19, Cambridge University Press 1971.

25. M. A. Utton, 'On Measuring the Effects of Industrial Mergers', *Scottish Journal of Political Economy*, 22, 1 February 1974.

26. Robert Jones, 'Where Have All the Merger Benefits Gone?', *The Statist*, October 2nd, 1964. The argument about overpriced acquisitions was based entirely on the fact that many breweries had been bought on an earnings yield basis of around 5 per cent or even less, when conventional opinion on the stock exchange held that a yield of 7.4 per cent was desirable for breweries. The author, however, neglected to mention the problem of under-valued assets.

27. In the case of Bass Mitchells and Butlers, for example, very little progress towards integration was made until after the death of the chairman, Sir James Grigg, in 1963. Until then the two constituent parts of the group continued to operate as more or less autonomous units. The difficulties in the way of integration were even more acute in the case of Charrington United Breweries, primarily because there was no geographical overlap between the two constituent halves of the group.

28. Whitbread, for example, are currently planning to build a 1.6 million barrel plant near Newport; Courage intends to build a similar-sized brewery at Reading,

while Bass, Allied and the Harp Lager consortium will almost certainly continue to expand their existing capacity over the next few years — see *Financial Times*, 29 March 1976.

29. One of the few examples of immediate and vigorous post-merger rationalisation occurred after Ind Coope's acquisition of Taylor Walker, when the latter's brewery was closed and only one product bearing its name (*Nourishing Stout*) was left on the market.

30. N.B.P.I., Report No. 13, p. 10.

31. Price Commission, op. cit., p. 4, para. 1.12

32. Monopolies Commission, op. cit., p. 92, para. 326.

33. Economists' Advisory Group, *The Economics of Brewing*, E.A.G., 1969. The survey covered thirteen areas where most licensed houses were thought to be under the control of one brewer. In fact it was found that in five of the thirteen areas, the leading brewer owned fewer than 40 per cent of the houses, while in four more the leading company owned between 40 per cent and 60 per cent. Only one area revealed a concentration level of over 80 per cent. These figures, of course, apply to public houses only. The range of choice both between places to drink and between the products of different brewers was, of course, considerably greater when clubs and other free trade outlets were taken into account.

34. Monopolies Commission, op. cit., p.99.

35. Exchanging licensed houses is not, of course, a straight-forward matter. Quite apart from the need to maintain efficient distribution systems and the problem of valuing each property, the interests of employees, licensees and customers are all involved. Nevertheless, in 1970 Courage and Trumans exchanged a total of 100 houses, and in 1971 Courage and Watney exchanged 150 houses in Bristol and Norwich. In 1977 Bass, Courage and Allied exchanged 437 houses.

36. Christopher Hutt, *The Death of the Eng-*

lish Pub, Arrow Books, 1973, p. 20.

37. It is ironic that bottled beer, which Mr. Hutt hardly ever mentions, is in fact more heavily carbonated than keg bitter or lager. One further point which should be noted is that usually the distinction between cask and keg beer is too sharply drawn. It tends to ignore the increasing significance of 'top pressure' or 'bright' beer, which lies between the two. Top pressure beer is conventional draught beer which is given sufficient filtration to remove the proteins and the yeast and is then lightly carbonated. Keg beer is filtered more severely and is more heavily carbonated. Some drinkers who profess to dislike keg beer still find top pressure beer very much to their taste; indeed sometimes they cannot distinguish it from cask beer.

38. In many breweries (including some of the smaller ones) a given beer will be produced in three separate forms, namely in cask, tank, and keg. Bass North, for example, produce *Brew Ten* in cask, tank and keg. The original gravity remains constant but the character of the beer may vary slightly according to whether it is dispensed from a cask or from a keg. Even so, a well-produced keg beer can yield as much flavour and taste as the same brand of beer in cask form.

39. Bass Charrington's policy is a case in point. Instead of concentrating exclusively on the two principal national brands (*Worthington E* and *Carling Black Label*), the group's regional concerns retained their own range of draught and bottled beers. Most of the draught beers were distributed in both cask and keg form. Where local loyalties were especially strong (as in Sheffield, where the popularity of *Stones'* was, and remains, immense) local beers have been retained. In addition, the company has developed a range of new beers specifically to cater for differences in regional tastes — *Brew 11*, for example was introduced into the Midlands in 1963, and *Brew 10*, into Yorkshire and the North East in 1970.

40. Hutt, op. cit., p. 129.

41. Report on the Departmental Committee on Liquor Licensing, HMSO, Cmnd, 5154, 1972, p. 61.

6 The Industry, 'Workable Competition', and the Public Interest

1. There were two partial exceptions to this general rule. One was the emergence of a handful of 'trust' companies (principally Trust Houses and the P.R.H.A.) who sought to prove (unsuccessfully) that the key to the industry's future survival lay in the principle of 'disinterested management'. These companies made a very limited entry into the retail trade through the purchase of licensed houses but never attempted to penetrate the wholesale side of the industry. The second exception was the development of a very small number of 'club' breweries, i.e. regional firms whose sole market is comprised of registered clubs. The exclusive function of these breweries has always been to supply the club trade, within which they compete with other brewers, but they have never moved beyond this section of the retail market. No 'club' brewery has been established since 1921.

2. Grand Metropolitan, for example, paid £50 million for Truman and £405 million for Watney Mann, which made the latter the most expensive purchase ever seen in the UK.

3. The most conspicuous example of 'imported' professionalism was that of Truman in 1969-71, when a completely new management team came into the firm from other industries and had begun to achieve a real transformation in its performance when Grand Metropolitan made a take-over bid.

4. Report of the Departmental Committee on Liquor Licensing, Cmnd. 5154;

HMSO, December 1972, p. 79, para. 8.09.

5. Ibid., p. 88.

6. Ibid., p. 65, para. 5.23.

7. Monopolies Commission, op. cit., p. 119, para. 4.16.

8. See Monopolies Commission, op. cit., p. 37 and Report of Departmental Committee etc., 1972, p. 85. These statistics show that in the period 1962-71, 85-90 per cent of all applications for new full on-licences (mainly public houses) were successful. The success rate for off-licences increased over this period from about 75 per cent in 1962-66 to around 85 per cent in the early 1970s.

9. Report of Departmental Committee, on Liquor Licensing, op. cit., pp. 60-3.

10. Ibid., pp. 136-62. The main proposal advanced by the committee was that a licencee be permitted to sell liquor for on-consumption at any time between 10.00 a.m. and 12 midnight. This was qualified by a further proposal that the licensing justices (acting in the interests of public order, safety, health or amenity) should be given the right to order licensees to close their premises for two consecutive hours in the period leading up to 7.00 p.m. and also to order licensees (on similar grounds) to close between 10.00 p.m. and 12 midnight. The Committee emphasised, however, that the provision of flexible hours of sale would not necessarily lead to a major increase in aggregate hours.

11. Ibid., p. 90, para. 8.34.

12. Ibid., p. 87, para. 8.31.

13. Ibid., p. 262, para. 21.27.

14. Ibid., p. 89, para. 8.33.

15. A similar position would apply in the case of soft drinks and cheap branded table wines where the national brewers have successfully established their own brands in the free trade over the past decade.

16. Report of Departmental Committee on Liquor Licensing, p. 261, para. 21.23.

17. Monopolies Commission, op. cit., p. 94, para. 333.

18. D. Swann, D. P. O'Brien, W. P. J. Maunder, W. S. Howe, *Competition in British Industry*, Allen and Unwin 1974, p. 119.

19. E. H. Chamberlin, *The Theory of Monopolistic Competition*, Cambridge University Press, 1933, Chapter 3.

20. Vaizey, op. cit., pp. 158-9.

21. The managing director of T. & R. Theakston & Co. Ltd. has been quoted as saying of his own firm's policy in this field: 'We have sold pubs which were not paying their way because we would much prefer to put money into those which show a good return', *The Financial Times* 24 April 1974.

22. Swann, *et al.*, op. cit., p. 128.

23. G. J. Stigler, Extent and Bases of Monopoly', *American Economic Review*, June 1942.

24. Vaizey, op. cit., p. 164.

25. Erroll Committee, p. 257, para. 21.18.

26. J. W. Markham, *Competition in the Rayon Industry*, Harvard University Press 1952, p. 204.

Index